BLAKE'S

Comprehension Guide

for primary students

Del Merrick

PASCAL
PRESS

Blake's Comprehension Guide

Copyright © 2014 Blake Education & Del Merrick
Reprinted 2015, 2017

ISBN: 978 1 92222 542 9

Published by Pascal Press
PO Box 250
Glebe NSW 2037
www.pascalpress.com.au
contact@pascalpress.com.au

Author: Del Merrick
Publisher: Lynn Dickinson
Editor: Vanessa Barker
Design and illustration: Janice Bowles
Printed by Green Giant Press

CONTENTS

CONTENTS continued...

CONTENTS continued...

AUSTRALIAN CURRICULUM CORRELATIONS - YEAR 3

LANGUAGE	ELABORATIONS	ACELA	PAGE
Text structure and organisation			
Understand how different types of texts vary in use of language choices, depending on their purpose and context (for example, tense and types of sentences)	• becoming familiar with typical structural stages and language features of various types of text, for example narratives, procedures, reports, reviews and expositions	1478	9, 35–36, 61, 66, 70, 74, 79, 83
Understand that paragraphs are a key organisational feature of written texts	• noticing how longer texts are organised into paragraphs, each beginning with a topic sentence/paragraph opener which predicts how the paragraph will develop and is then elaborated in various ways	1479	9, 44, 58–60, 62–63, 75, 80
Expressing and developing ideas			
Identify the effect on audiences of techniques, for example shot size, vertical camera angle and layout in picture books, advertisements and film segments	• noting how the relationship between characters can be depicted in illustrations through: the positioning of the characters (for example facing each other or facing away from each other); the distance between them; the relative size; one character looking up (or down) at the other (power relationships); facial expressions and body gesture	1483	3, 8, 10, 15, 20, 49–50

LITERACY		ACELY	
Texts in context			
Identify the point of view in a text and suggest alternative points of view	• discussing how a text presents the point of view of the main character, and speculating on what other characters might think or feel	1675	2, 61, 79–85
Interpreting, analysing, evaluating			
Identify the audience and purpose of imaginative, informative and persuasive texts	• identifying the author's point of view on a topic and key words and images that seem intended to persuade listeners, viewers or readers to agree with the view presented	1678	2, 61, 77–79, 83
Read an increasing range of different types of texts by combining contextual, semantic, grammatical and phonic knowledge, using text processing strategies, for example monitoring, predicting, confirming, rereading, reading on and self-correcting	• combining different types of knowledge (for example word knowledge, vocabulary, grammar, phonics) to make decisions about unknown words, reading on, reviewing and summarising meaning • analysing the way illustrations help to construct meaning and interpreting different types of illustrations and graphics	1679	10–13, 38–40, 53–54
Use comprehension strategies to build literal and inferred meaning and begin to evaluate texts by drawing on a growing knowledge of context, text structures and language features	• making connections between the text and students own experience and other texts • making connections between the information in print and images • making predictions and asking and answering questions about the text drawing on knowledge of the topic, subject-specific vocabulary and experience of texts on the same topic • using text features and search tools to locate information in written and digital texts efficiently • determining important ideas, events or details in texts commenting on things learned or questions raised by reading, referring explicitly to the text for verification • making considered inferences taking into account topic knowledge or a character's likely actions and feelings	1680	16, 18–21, 23, 26, 36, 37, 38, 44, 52–86

AUSTRALIAN CURRICULUM CORRELATIONS - YEAR 4

LANGUAGE	ELABORATIONS	ACELA	PAGE
Text structure and organisation			
Understand how texts vary in complexity and technicality depending on the approach to the topic, the purpose and the intended audience	• becoming familiar with the typical stages and language features of such text types as: simple narrative, procedure, simple persuasion texts and information reports	1490	23–26, 35–36, 61, 66, 70, 74, 79, 83
Understand how texts are made cohesive through the use of linking devices including pronoun reference and text connectives	• knowing how authors construct texts that are cohesive and coherent through the use of: pronouns that link to something previously mentioned; determiners (for example 'this', 'that', 'these', 'those', 'the',); text connectives that create links between sentences (for example 'however', 'therefore', 'nevertheless', 'in addition', 'by contrast', 'in summary') • identifying how participants are tracked through a text by, for example, using pronouns to refer back to noun groups/phrases • describing how text connectives link sections of a text providing sequences through time, for example 'firstly', 'then', 'next', and 'finally'	1491	19, 23–34, 40–41, 43

LANGUAGE	ELABORATIONS	ACELA	PAGE
Expressing and developing ideas			
Explore the effect of choices when framing an image, placement of elements in the image, and salience on composition of still and moving images in a range of types of texts	• examining visual and multimodal texts, building a vocabulary to describe visual elements and techniques such as framing, composition and visual point of view and beginning to understand how these choices impact on viewer response	1496	10–14, 50
LITERACY		**ACELY**	
Interpreting, analysing, evaluating			
Identify characteristic features used in imaginative, informative and persuasive texts to meet the purpose of the text	• describing the language which authors use to create imaginary worlds; how textual features such as headings, subheadings, bold type and graphic organisers are used to order and present information, and how visual codes are used, for example those used in advertising to represent children and families so that viewers identify with them	1690	3, 10, 53–55, 86, 87
Read different types of texts by combining contextual, semantic, grammatical and phonic knowledge using text processing strategies for example monitoring meaning, cross checking and reviewing	• reading new and different kinds of texts with the use of established word identification strategies, including knowledge of the topic and of text type together with self monitoring strategies; including rereading, self questioning and pausing, and including self correction strategies such confirming and cross-checking	1691	16, 40, 56
Use comprehension strategies to build literal and inferred meaning to expand content knowledge, integrating and linking ideas and analysing and evaluating texts	• making connections between the text and students' own experience and other texts • making connections between information in print and images • building and using prior knowledge and vocabulary • finding specific literal information • asking and answering questions • creating mental images • finding the main idea of a text • inferring meaning from the ways communication occurs in digital environments including the interplay between words, images, and sounds	1692	8, 18, 19, 37, 38, 39, 45, 57–58, 61, 65, 69, 71, 72, 76, 77, 78, 81, 85

AUSTRALIAN CURRICULUM CORRELATIONS - YEAR 5

LANGUAGE	ELABORATIONS	ACELA	PAGE
Text structure and organisation			
Understand how texts vary in purpose, structure and topic as well as the degree of formality	• becoming familiar with the typical stages and language features of such text types as: narrative, procedure, exposition, explanation, discussion and informative text and how they can be composed and presented in written, digital and multimedia forms	1504	16, 17, 23–26, 35–46, 61–84
LITERATURE		**ACELT**	
Examining literature			
Understand, interpret and experiment with sound devices and imagery, including simile, metaphor and personification, in narratives, shape poetry, songs, anthems and odes	• discussing how figurative language including simile and metaphor can make use of a comparison between different things, for example 'My love is like a red, red rose'; 'Tyger!, Tyger! burning bright, In the forests of the night'; and how by appealing to the imagination, it provides new ways of looking at the world	1611	5, 6, 7, 46
LITERACY		**ACELY**	
Interpreting, analysing, evaluating			
Identify and explain characteristic text structures and language features used in imaginative, informative and persuasive texts to meet the purpose of the text	• explaining how the features of a text advocating community action, for example action on a local area preservation issue, are used to meet the purpose of the text	1701	79–82, 83–85

LITERACY		ACELY	PAGE
Interpreting, analysing, evaluating			
Navigate and read texts for specific purposes applying appropriate text processing strategies, for example predicting and confirming, monitoring meaning, skimming and scanning	• bringing subject and technical vocabulary and concept knowledge to new reading tasks • selecting and using texts for their pertinence to the task and the accuracy of their information • using word identification, self-monitoring and self-correcting strategies to access material on less familiar topics, skimming and scanning to check the pertinence of particular information to students' topic and task	1702	4, 38, 40, 45, 56–58, 61, 64, 78
Use comprehension strategies to analyse information, integrating and linking ideas from a variety of print and digital sources	• using research skills including identifying research, purpose, locating texts, gathering and organising information, evaluating its relative value, and summarising information from several sources	1703	56, 77–78, 86, 87

AUSTRALIAN CURRICULUM CORRELATIONS - YEAR 6

LANGUAGE	ELABORATIONS	ACELA	PAGE
Text structure and organisation			
Understand that cohesive links can be made in texts by omitting or replacing words	• noting how a general word is often used for a more specific word already mentioned, for example 'Look at those apples. Can I have one?' • recognising how cohesion can be developed through repeating key words or by using synonyms or antonyms • observing how relationships between concepts can be represented visually through similarity, contrast, juxtaposition, repetition, class-subclass diagrams, part-whole diagrams, cause-and-effect figures, visual continuities and discontinuities	1520	10, 29, 32, 33, 53–55, 86, 87
Expressing and developing ideas			
Identify and explain how analytical images like figures, tables, diagrams, maps and graphs contribute to our understanding of verbal information in factual and persuasive texts	• observing how sequential events can be represented visually by a series of images, including comic strips, timelines, photo stories, procedure diagrams and flowcharts, life-cycle diagrams, and the flow of images in picture books • observing how concepts, information and relationships can be represented visually through such images as tables, maps, graphs, diagrams, and icons	1524	53–55, 75, 76, 86, 87

LITERACY		ACELY	
Interpreting, analysing, evaluating			
Analyse how text structures and language features work together to meet the purpose of a text	• comparing the structures and features of different texts, including print and digital sources on similar topics, and evaluating which features best aid navigation and clear communication about the topic	1711	9, 23–26, 35, 61, 66, 70, 74, 79, 83
Select, navigate and read texts for a range of purposes, applying appropriate text processing strategies and interpreting structural features, for example table of contents, glossary, chapters, headings and subheadings	• using word identification, self-monitoring and self-correcting strategies • using research skills including identifying research purpose, locating texts, gathering and organising information, evaluating and using information	1712	17, 56–58, 85
Use comprehension strategies to interpret and analyse information and ideas, comparing content from a variety of textual sources including media and digital texts	• making connections between the text and students' own experience or other texts • making connections between information in print and images • finding specific literal information • using prior knowledge and textual information to make inferences and predictions • asking and answering questions • finding the main idea of a text • summarising a text or part of a text	1713	18, 35–49, 53–87

HOW TO USE THIS BOOK

Blake's Comprehension Guide has been written to give you clear insights into how we make meaning from text. It has two parts:

- **Part 1** gives a detailed explanation of the comprehending process and the ways we make meaning from printed, spoken and visual texts.

- **Part 2** contains detailed explanations of how texts 'work' and elaborates on a broad range of practical strategies you can use to help you make meaning from different types of text.

Explanations, definitions, examples and **Try This** activities are included throughout the book to help you better understand new ideas and gather knowledge about how we make meaning through our language.

The Guide also contains an index and a glossary of terms for quick reference.

ABOUT the AUTHOR

Del has enjoyed a long career in education as a specialist teacher (Learning Difficulties), education adviser and regional coordinator (English). She has written extensively for parents, teachers and students, and is a well-known and respected author nationally and internationally. Her publications cover a diverse range of print and electronic materials for English grammar, spelling, reading, writing and comprehension. Among her latest works for primary students are *Blake's Grammar and Punctuation Guide* and *Targeting Spelling*, a comprehensive spelling program.

INTRODUCTION

When you think about it, we are constantly **making meaning** — constantly 'reading' the world around us so that we can understand it and learn how to live in it. Through **language** we learn about others and ourselves: how to communicate, how to behave and how to belong.

We learn about the world by listening to others, and through **reading** and **viewing** texts. We are constantly receiving and absorbing new information. This shapes what we think and believe, and how we behave.

When we read, we take on the role of a detective — a problem-solver — and we use a range of strategies to discover the meaning of a text. Like any detective, we'll start with what we know; we'll gather bits of information, ask questions and make connections. We'll consider important details, draw conclusions and, finally, make a personal evaluation of what we've read. The meaning we make from a text is our personal interpretation. Others may have a different 'take' on things.

This book will take you on a fact-finding mission into learning more about comprehension and the strategies we use to unlock meaning.

Enjoy the journey!

Del Merrick

WHY DO WE READ?

Language reflects and shapes our culture and lifestyle, and helps us make sense of our world. Through reading and viewing texts, we can also live in worlds outside our experience: in our imagination, in times past, in the present and in possible futures.

We have three main reasons for reading and viewing texts:

- We read for ENJOYMENT (stories, video games, movies, cartoons, comics, poems).
- We read to MAKE or DO something (follow instructions, directions or procedures).
- We read to find and use INFORMATION (books, websites, advertisements, TV guides).

Most texts are supported by visuals (pictures, photos, drawings). Words, images and sounds (speech, music and sound effects) work closely together to make meaning.

WHAT IS TEXT?

Writers, composers, filmmakers and artists use words, pictures and symbols to create texts that capture and explain the world — the world of the every day and the world of the imagination. They give voice to ideas, events, truths and opinions about the world as they see it. They write from their own knowledge, beliefs and experience (point of view), often called the author's stance. As readers, we also come to a text with our own personal point of view. This is our reader's stance and it will always affect the meaning we make from a text.

(See How do we make meaning? pp. 2–3)

Texts have many faces and may consist of:

- words, books, plays, cartoons and caricatures
- photos, pictures, sketches and paintings
- movies and animated cartoons
- graphs, diagrams, cutaways and timelines
- signs and symbols.

Many texts are created using a combination of these elements. A good example is television, which generally brings together spoken, written, non-verbal, visual and auditory language. These texts are called **multimodal texts**.

WHAT IS CONTEXT?

The context is the setting or situation in which language occurs.

Social context

We are all members of different **social groups** — our family, class, football team or choir. We use language to communicate with each other, to build our relationships and to conduct our everyday lives. We choose language that is appropriate for each situation (context) we find ourselves in.

Speakers, writers, producers and artists consider:

WHAT they want to 'say'— the subject or topic

WHY they want to say it — their purpose

WHO their text is for (students, doctors, athletes, scientists, migrants) and the relationship between the writer and reader, speaker and listener, producer and viewer

WHICH type of language they'll use (spoken, written, visual, multimodal, non-verbal)

HOW they'll deliver the text (email, phone, book, movie, text message, magazine).

These factors make up the context.

Cultural context

Not only are we members of different social groups, we also belong to a much larger **cultural group** — for example, Australian, Chinese, Indian, Iranian and so on. Every culture has developed its own ways of doing things.

Our **culture** influences how we think, feel and act; and how we interact with others. We learn how to behave and how to use our language to get things done. We learn to do certain things in certain ways, such as ordering food at a restaurant; shopping at a supermarket; catching a bus, train or plane; attending a football game or concert; or growing food. These activities may be done differently, or not at all, in some cultures. Some things we do and say in one culture may not be acceptable in another.

WHAT IS COMPREHENSION?

When we read a book, we are *making meaning*, not just saying the words.
When we watch TV, we are *making meaning*, not just seeing images on a screen. When we listen to speech, we are *making meaning*, not just hearing words.

Comprehension is our ability to make meaning from text.

At a basic level, we understand the meanings of words within the context of the words nearby and the grammar that ties them together.

For example, the word **close** means different things in different contexts:

- Please, *close* the door.
- He is a *close* friend of my dad's.
- The event will *close* with a fireworks display.
- Jane was *close* to fainting in the hot, stuffy room.
- Edward is *close* to the front of the line.
- The workmen may need to *close* off the street.
- The police will soon *close* in on the suspect.
- The government called for a *close* study of marine life on the reef.

We live in a meaning-making world!

Words and images are the tools that carry the message. When we read (or view) a text, we understand:

- its purpose (why it has been created)
- what it's about
- who is involved
- what it looks like
- how it 'works'.

Mmmm! What do I know about this?

Information in the text

Your understanding is coloured by what you know and believe about the topic, and what attitudes you have developed from past experiences in your life.

HOW DO WE MAKE MEANING?

To make meaning from text, we use information from two sources:

1. the information in the text
2. the store of knowledge we have in our head and our past experiences.

Text information

At the heart of reading is the **text** that has been created:

- for a particular purpose — *to explain or show you how to do something, to make you laugh, or to persuade you to do or buy something*
- from a particular point of view — *the author's stance*
- for a particular audience — *young children, scientists, gardeners, cyclists*
- in a particular context — *the What, Who, Which and How*
- in a particular way — *its structure, vocabulary, grammar and other features.*

Reader resources

At the heart of reading is also the **reader**, who comes to the text with:

- a specific purpose in mind
- beliefs and attitudes developed through past experiences
- knowledge about the topic
- knowledge of how texts 'work'
- a range of strategies to unlock meaning.

Example:

These children are reading about submarines.

Great! I know a lot about subs!

Oooh, I'd hate to be trapped in one of these!

Dad and I made a model sub like this. Cool!

Boring! I think I'll skip these pages.

**Think about how *you* make meaning from this text.
Use the questions to help you.**

Hey, Tom. We're going snorkelling on the Barrier Reef these holidays.

Lucky you, DJ! Dad wants to go birdwatching! Again!

- How do you know this text is spoken?
- How do you know it's a conversation between two boys?
- How do you know the boys are friends rather than strangers?
- Why does Tom call the other boy DJ?
- Who speaks first?
- What are they talking about?
- Where is the *Barrier Reef*? What is *snorkelling*? How do you know that?
- How does DJ feel about his holiday?
- How does Tom feel about his holiday?
- Which holiday would you choose? Why?

Try *this*

To make meaning you need to understand the cultural and social context.

COMPREHENDING WORDS

Through their choice of **vocabulary**, authors give life and personality to the people and things they speak and write about. The words they choose build pictures in our mind and influence the way we view things.

For example, we get to like or dislike the characters in a story by the way the author describes them and what they do. The illustrations in the story support this view.

The **white** knight is most often described as *handsome, brave* or *strong*. He performs deeds that are *courageous, noble* and *compassionate*.

The **black** knight, on the other hand, is often described as *arrogant, mean* and *sinister*. He performs deeds that are *violent, ruthless* or *vicious*.

THE AUTHOR'S TOOLKIT

Words are the tools authors use to build a text. Their tools include the following:

Nouns

Nouns are the words that name the people, places, animals and things in a text. An author usually writes with an audience in mind, choosing words carefully so they can be understood. Problems with comprehension arise when the reader doesn't understand the author's words.

As readers, we need to be aware that some texts, such as science reports, will contain 'technical' vocabulary rather than the 'everyday' language of recounts, emails and diary entries.

Adjectives

Adjectives give colour and texture to nouns and build clear pictures in the mind of the reader.

They depict:

- shape *(round, oval, square)*
- size *(large, tiny, towering)*
- sound *(loud, noisy, silent)*
- colour *(red, yellow, olive green)*
- mood *(sullen, angry, excited)*
- personal characteristics *(clumsy, stubborn, popular)*.

Verbs

Verbs tie ideas together in a text. They create strong images of movement, action and behaviour.

They show:

- what people and things are doing *(fly, sleep, swim, cry, dance, eat, trickle)*
- how people express themselves *(whisper, shout, squeal, whimper, blubber, growl)*
- how people process ideas *(believe, remember, imagine, ponder, reminisce, think)*.

They include:

- being verbs *(is, are, was, were, be, being, been)*
- having verbs *(has, have, had)*.

Characters are brought to life through vocabulary!

Adverbs

Adverbs add meaning to the actions of people, places, objects and events.

They tell us:

- how something is being done (*anxiously, slowly, warily, quickly, happily*)
- when things are happening (*yesterday, now, tomorrow, soon, later*)
- how often things are happening (*seldom, usually, twice, occasionally*)
- where things are happening (*here, there, everywhere, away*).

Adverbs give a positive feel to text with words like *certainly, yes, undoubtedly* and *surely*. They give a sense of possibility with words like *maybe, perhaps, possibly* and *probably*.

The adverb **not** is used to negate a positive statement.

far, *not* far.   You should go. You should *not* go.

It is often written with a verb as a contraction.

do *not* = *don't*   could *not* = *couldn't*   is *not* = *isn't*

Figurative language

Authors create images in our minds by using words and phrases whose meanings are often **implied** rather than **literal**. (See Three levels of comprehension p. 18) These expressions — called **figures of speech** — add colour, interest and often humour to our everyday language.

Here are some examples:

Similes

Similes are phrases that say how one thing is like, or similar to, another thing. The phrase usually begins with *like* or *as*. The meaning is **implied** rather than literal. Similes are very common in both spoken and written text.

Example: *My love for you is as deep as the ocean and as wide as the sky.*

Similes paint vivid pictures in the mind of the reader.

Compare: *"He burst into the room, his face as black as thunder."*
to *"He burst into the room angrily."*

Try this

Find the similes in these sentences. Think about the meanings behind the words.

1. Run like the wind, Marco.
2. I felt like a fish out of water at the party.
3. The leaves under his feet were as crisp as cornflakes.
4. His eyes were like saucers and his face was as white as a sheet.

Metaphors

Metaphors are terms and phrases that do not represent the literal truth. In other words, they don't mean exactly what they say. The truth lies in their **implied meaning**.

(See Inferential comprehension p. 19)

For example, if you give someone the 'green light', you are not handing them a green torch or lantern. You are giving them permission to go ahead with something. We understand this because we know that a green traffic light always means 'go' to a driver.

Metaphors are in common use everywhere, every day, in spoken and written text. They add richness, clarity and depth of meaning.

Try this

What are the true meanings of these sentences?

1. The thief was caught red-handed.
    He had red paint on his hands.
    He was caught committing a crime.

2. I'm afraid Jones doesn't have a leg to stand on.
    Jones doesn't have any acceptable excuses.
    Jones has lost his legs.

3. OK Benson, time to pull your socks up!
    Benson's socks are probably wrinkled and he needs to pull them up.
    It's time Benson made a greater effort.

Metaphors are fun to explore. These metaphors are built around parts of the body. Can you add some more?

- To step on someone's toes
- To have itchy feet
- To keep your ear to the ground
- To get your fingers burnt
- To stand on your own two feet
- To get cold feet
- To scratch your head
- To keep your head above water
- To be head and shoulders above
- To twist someone's arm

Try this

Euphemisms

Euphemisms are deliberately vague or polite expressions used to describe things that may be embarrassing, unpleasant or awkward.

Example:
When someone has died, we might say he has 'passed away', 'gone to a better place' or is 'resting in peace'.

Personification

Personification is a technique authors use to make animals and objects appear human to the reader. The author might give animals proper names and use 'he' and 'she' rather than 'it'. They might use verbs and adverbs usually associated with human behaviour, or give their animal characters human feelings. As a result, readers are able to engage more closely with the characters.

Authors may also use personification to humanise non-living things. It is a technique often used in poetry.

Example:

Mountains rise from the dark of night

Kissed by the first flush of morning

Shadows melt into moss and lichen

While far below, a silent fjord lies dreaming

Under a blood-red sky

Example:

"We heard what happened, Lulu," Lounge Lizard said sadly.

"Yeah. Tough luck, I say," complained Basso, her noisy bullfrog friend.

"But we're here to help," Lounge said, looking cheerful again.

"Do you have a plan?" Lulu asked, eyeing her friends doubtfully.

Leghorn-Lou strutted forward. "Ab-so-lute-ly!" he said, tail feathers waggling and copper top bristling.

Puns

A **pun** is a clever or humorous play on words. All you need are a couple of words that have different meanings or spellings — and a sense of humour of course!

Examples:

Did you hear about the man who had his whole left side cut off? He's all right now.

The noisy plumber was told to pipe down.

I couldn't quite remember how to throw a boomerang, but eventually it came back to me.

10 Egg-citing things to do at Easter

One-armed man applauds the kindness of strangers

(For further information, see *Blake's Guide to English* by Peter Clutterbuck.)

COMPREHENDING SPOKEN TEXTS

We make meaning from spoken language by listening not only to the words, but to the sound of the speaker's voice. A speaker's voice generally rises and falls in pitch (tone) as they speak. This rhythmic way of speaking is also known as **cadence**.

Both the **pitch** and the **volume** tend to rise when the speaker is excited or agitated, and fall when the speaker is uncertain, intimate or secretive. To make meaning clear to listeners, the speaker will often slow his or her rate of speech, pause for effect, or emphasise or repeat words.

Example:

"You must never, NEVER, do that again! If you do, I'll ... I'll make you pay, BIG time!"

We can learn a lot by observing changes in the speaker's **tone of voice**.

Of course we can only understand what is being said if the speaker **enunciates** his or her words clearly, speaks **fluently** and with a good sense of timing — not too fast and not too slow. It is difficult to make meaning from mumbled, poorly articulated or garbled speech.

When we can see the speaker, we also make meaning by closely observing the speaker's facial expressions, hand gestures and **body language**.

(See Comprehending non-verbal texts p.15)

Quite often a speaker is saying one thing but body language is saying another!

You want to go mud wrestling?

In **face-to-face encounters**, we usually take turns at speaking and listening.

Because we usually have a shared understanding of the context, we are able to leave out or substitute words and still be understood.

Examples:

"I'm having coffee. Want some?"

"Where did you see the dog?"   "In front of Bill's."

"Everyone's heading to the final. Wanna come?"

We frequently use **colloquialisms**, **slang** or street language in everyday or **informal** speech.

Example:

"Keep ya shirt on, Fred! Sid's just gone bush for a while. Between you and me and the gatepost, he can get lost for all I care!"

COMPREHENDING PRINTED TEXTS

Reading books and printed materials requires you to move your eyes from left to right, line by line, down the page, from the beginning to the end. As you read, you **make meaning** through the words, pictures and sentences.

The sentences contain complete ideas — these ideas are linked together by the writer, so that you construct meaning while you are reading. What you already know about the topic also helps you to make meaning.

Many things help you make meaning on the way:

- format — *what the text looks like*

- layout — *how the text is arranged on the page*

- understanding the way the text is organised

- understanding the words and the way grammar ties them together

- understanding how one idea links to another

- punctuation marks, headings, subheadings and paragraphs

- any illustrations that support the text

- a dictionary to check the meanings of unfamiliar words.

Making meaning is like rolling a snowball. It starts with what you know and grows as you gather in more and more information.

A dictionary is a reader's best friend!

COMPREHENDING VISUAL TEXTS

In visual language, an **image** is a representation of reality produced by a photographer, artist or illustrator. These images may be still images (photos, illustrations, paintings, icons or graphic representations) or moving images (movies, animations or live streams).

Still images
Illustrations

Illustrators depict scenes from a story to clarify or extend the meaning. Their **illustrations** are an artistic expression of their interpretation of the story and add significant value to the author's words. They show where the events take place, what the characters look like and how they are feeling. They add to the overall mood of a story by creating pictures that are humorous or lifelike, whimsical or serious, scary, and so on.

Usually words and pictures go together to make meaning. Sometimes, such as when there are very few words, the pictures carry most of the meaning.

A text could be illustrated in different ways to show different meanings.

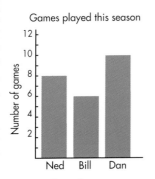

Jack forgot his homework.

Graphic representations

Graphic designers present information in visual form through **graphic representations** (graphs, timelines, cutaways, labelled sketches and diagrams) to summarise and clarify information. These types of images are found in many information and procedural texts, and greatly add to the reader's understanding.

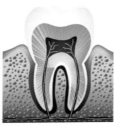

Graph

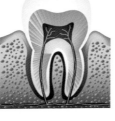

Cutaway

Flow chart

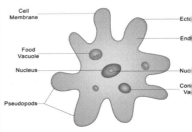

Labelled diagram

Photographs

Photographers use cameras to produce still images in the form of **photographs** (photos).

Photos have certain features that influence the way we 'read' them. These include:

- **subject** — *person, object, animal*
- **composition** — *the placement of the subject in the frame. Subjects may be photographed in close-up, portrait or landscape. The people or objects in the centre and foreground are usually of main interest. Other people or objects in the background provide the context. Colour (including black-and-white and* **sepia***), shapes, shadows and highlights are also important elements of composition.*
- **medium** — *film (35 mm, colour, black and white, instant) or digital (digital cameras, phone cameras, photo apps and filters)*
- **type of lens used** — *normal, close-up, fish-eye, wide-angle*
- **camera angle** — *eye level, high, low, wide, bird's-eye view*
- **type of light** (to give different mood effects) — *bright, soft, side, backlit.*

  sepia: a brownish colour, used to make photos look 'old'

Some photos are **personal** and **informal**. These are photos taken at family outings, birthdays and special events. They are most meaningful to the people involved.

Other photos are more carefully planned to show the subject in a certain way. The subject is carefully framed, often in the **foreground**, with related objects in the **background** to add context and meaning.

Like any other text, photos are produced within the wider **social and cultural context**. Magazine designers, news editors and advertisers use a range of different techniques to present images in positive or negative ways. Many photos are designed for a particular purpose, such as to persuade us to buy an item or a particular brand of something, to choose a holiday destination, or to try a new recipe.

(See What is context? p. xii)

Fish-eye

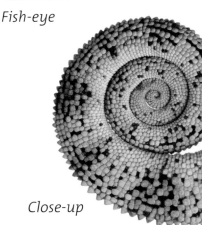

Close-up

Bird's-eye view

To make meaning from a photo, we need to understand its **context**, its **purpose**, and the way it has been composed and produced.

Signs

Signs are a means of giving information to a large audience in such a way that everyone can understand it.

They are a type of sign language, a shortcut to meaning, much like icons on a computer screen. Many signs have no words so everyone can easily understand them, regardless of the language they speak. We depend on signs to help us navigate our public spaces.

Written signs are used to send messages to the general public in many situations. For example, in shops we may see the following signs:

Please do not touch

Try this

Look around you and you will see that there are signs everywhere! Check out how many you understand!

Can you read these signs?

Drivers rely on signs to ensure safe travel. Can you recognise these signs?

Symbols

A **symbol** is a mark or an image that represents something **conventional** ($ = money) or **abstract** (♥ = love).

Here are some familiar symbols:

peace   *recycling*   *music*   *bright idea*   *freedom*

Music is a language composed almost entirely of signs and symbols, and is recognised by musicians all over the world. To play a musical instrument from a score, the musician has to be able to read and understand the signs.

Examples of musical signs and symbols

Moving images

Moving images are created with video cameras or digicams (digital cameras). Filmmakers and TV cameramen use the same techniques as still photographers to compose their shots. They **shoot** scenes in short segments called **takes**, then join them together carefully in a process called **editing**.

Television programs and movies on the 'big screen' (cinema) are generally **multimodal texts**. They require us to move our eyes quickly all over the screen to make sense of the moving images. Multimodal texts require us to make meaning from several sources, all at the same time.

Examples:
- images on the screen — *actors, settings, animated characters, news reporters*
- movement — *action, non-verbal language*
- speech — *dialogue, narration, voice-over*
- music, lighting and sound effects — *to create different moods*
- subtitles — *for languages other than the native language; for hearing-impaired viewers.*

Television

Television programs, news reports and advertising are also multimodal texts, and place the same demands on the viewer as the big screen.

Some television stations provide on-screen information during programs by using a continuous flow of text across the bottom of the screen. This is called a **news ticker** or **crawler**, and shows the latest news items, sports results, weather forecasts and so on. During live sports events, the score appears on the screen and is constantly updated during play.

Because television reaches a very big audience, important news is flashed onto the screen as 'breaking news'. Viewers can receive updated storm, flood or fire warnings, and respond immediately if necessary.

Sometimes the screen is split into two or more segments, called a **split-screen**, with each showing different images. In a news report, for example, we often see the reporter in the foreground and images of the news item in the background.

Viewers can also 'channel surf' and access program guides using the menu button on the remote control.

Computers and tablets

Computers, **smartphones**, **tablets** like the iPad, and **e-readers** like the Kindle require us to scan through icons on a screen. We can use computers, tablets and smartphones to check emails, play games, watch videos and listen to music. We can also use them as cameras or camcorders. We use these devices to access websites, and to keep in touch with people via **social networking** sites such as Facebook and Twitter.

Tablets and smartphones have a **touchscreen**, and we sweep our fingers across the screen to locate the icon we need. We tap on the icon to open a program or **app** (application). An on-screen, pop-up keyboard can be used for typing. Some computers also have a touchscreen, replacing the need for a traditional keyboard and mouse.

COMPREHENDING NON-VERBAL TEXTS

In face-to-face encounters, we communicate in two ways — through **verbal language** (spoken) and **non-verbal language** (body language, gestures and facial expressions). Our postures, movements, gestures and facial expressions 'give away' what we really think, feel and believe about what is being said.

We are often unaware that we are doing this, but our non-verbal cues and signals form a very large part of the way we communicate and understand each other.

Deaf people use non-verbal **sign language** to communicate with others. They use finger spelling, hand shapes, gestures, body language and facial expressions to make meaning. During important national announcements on TV, a person who 'signs' the message for deaf viewers often accompanies the speaker.

What do these non-verbal signals tell you?

Try this

Aa Bb Cc Dd Ee Ff Gg

Hh Ii Jj Kk Ll Mm

Nn Oo Pp Qq Rr Ss

Tt Uu Vv Ww Xx Yy Zz

Blind people are able to read text through a system of raised dots called **braille**.

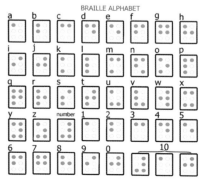

BRAILLE ALPHABET

a b c d e f g h
i j k l m n o p
q r s t u v w x
y z number 1 2 3 4 5
6 7 8 9 10

"PUSH BUTTON"
FOR PEDESTRIAN
WARNING LIGHTS
CROSS WITH CAUTION

THE ART OF READING FICTION

In the world of make-believe, anything is possible and we can experience it all by reading works of **fiction** — stories of the imagination. These stories take us on endless journeys through countless adventures, and we encounter extraordinary people along the way. Stories fill us with a rainbow of emotions like fear, excitement, surprise, horror and amazement.

When we read a book, we start at the beginning and read to the end. We step inside the covers and get lost in the pages. We live through events alongside the characters — feeling their joys, their sorrows, their hopes and fears. We see them encounter and resolve problems, until, finally, there is nothing left to say and we must close the book and say goodbye, taking with us feelings and memories that may have changed the way we view our world.

The reader/writer connection

A book is just a book, but when you open that book, you are setting off on a path of discovery laid down for you by the writer. Words are just words, but as you read them, the story unfolds in your imagination.

You could say that you and the writer are 'at opposite ends of the pencil'. You read the writer's words and you build a picture of the story. You create the characters, places and events. The story you read is the story you have created in your imagination. A friend reading the same book will create a different version, but you are both connected to the writer through the same words.

While you can be 'inside' the book creating your story, you can also be 'outside' looking at the characters and events from a distance, like an audience watching a movie. There will be characters that you like and characters that annoy you. You may think they are heroic, clumsy, clever or scary. You might laugh at them or feel anxious for them. You may hope they can get out of trouble, survive hardship or beat up the enemy. You will judge the characters and wonder how you yourself would behave or act in the same situation. Above all, you will probably wish for a happy ending! These feelings are all part of the drama of reading.

> Perhaps the real purpose of a story is to open our minds to the possibilities in life, to shape our ideas, trigger feelings and influence our actions. We are often transformed by what we read.

THE ART OF READING NON-FICTION

When we read **non-fiction texts** (also known as factual texts), we are usually focused on what it is we want to do or make, or what we want to know more about. It is our **purpose** that determines what and how we read. We can choose our own pathways through factual texts. We can start at the beginning, the end or anywhere in between.

When we read to find specific information, we can choose which part of the text to read by scanning the:

- contents page
- index
- headings
- images (often photos) and captions.

We might only read one section to find the **information** we need. Our research may lead us to find and compare similar information in other books or websites. During our research, we look for main ideas, check out details and make notes.

Many factual texts do require us to start at the beginning and to read the information in **sequence**. When we read **instructions**, for example, we generally glance through them first and gather what we need (materials or ingredients), then we follow the instructions carefully, step by step. We alternate between reading and doing. We often go back and read things two or three times to make sure we are following the instructions correctly.

Often, we simply pick and choose what parts of a text we will read.

Here are some common examples:

- In a **phone book** we look for a particular name. In a **dictionary**, we look for a certain word. We are helped by the fact that the names or words are listed alphabetically.

- We go **online** to locate websites that can answer questions we have or give us immediate information about a specific subject.

- In a **newspaper**, we may only read the headlines, the sports section, interesting news articles, the social pages, the TV guide and so on.

Whether it's a menu or a web search, we focus only on finding the information we need at the time.

We only read what we need!

AUSTRALIAN ANIMALS

Sam Black

Contents

The koala belongs to a special group of mammals called marsupials.

page 8

Our purpose determines what, how much and how deeply we read a text.

THREE LEVELS OF COMPREHENSION

When we read different texts, we make meaning at three levels:

1. literal
2. inferential
3. personal (evaluative).

GIVE WAY

1. Literal comprehension

At the **literal comprehension** level, the words are **explicit** — they mean what they say. Examples of this are road signs and shop signs.

When we read texts that explain how to make or do something, we want and expect the words to mean exactly what they say so that we don't make mistakes.

How to Make Jelly

Ingredients:
* One 80 g packet of jelly
* 1 cup of boiling water

Method:
1. Empty the packet of jelly crystals into a bowl.
2. Add a cup of boiling water.
3. Stir until the jelly crystals have dissolved.
4. Place the cooled jelly in the refrigerator for 4 hours until set.

At the literal level, information is explicitly in the text, right there 'on the page'. The words (or equivalent words) mean what they say and we focus on their accurate meaning.

Examples:
Pietro leads his donkey down the narrow mountain path to the fishing village. He has baskets of olives and nuts, yellow cheeses, jars of olive oil, and crab pots woven by his father.

Smoke billowed from the blazing building. Ten people escaped down the fire escape and gathered on the footpath. They watched as the firemen sprayed water from long hoses onto the flames. After an hour, the fire was out.

2. Inferential comprehension

At the **inferential comprehension** level, the meaning is **implied** — the words don't say exactly what they mean. We have to think about them and work out what they mean by using the **context** to help us. This is often called 'reading between the lines'.

Using pieces of information from the text, we draw on our own knowledge and our past experiences to derive meaning. It could be as simple as understanding that a **pronoun** stands in the place of a noun.

What words do these pronouns imply?

Lena's father enters the room. "Quickly Pytherius, Marco, **you** must get to the boat," **he** says softly. "**You** must get away before the sun comes up or the soldiers will see **you**."

Pytherius thanks **him** and the two men hurry to the boat, hoping the soldiers won't see **them**.

At the inferential level, we gather bits of information together and draw our own conclusions about the characters, what is happening and why.

Try this

What conclusions can you draw from these texts?

1. Outside in the dentist's waiting room, Tommy Tucker is shivering in his socks.

    He feels cold.

    He feels nervous.

2. Little Alfie stared at the man, wide-eyed, his heart beating fast. He opened his mouth to speak but no words came out.

    He was very frightened.

    He had been running and couldn't catch his breath.

3. The first rays of sun are chasing away the shadows in Sam's room.

    The shadows are running out of the room.

    The room is becoming brighter.

In many face-to-face encounters, much of the meaning is implied. We often read between the lines to make meaning.

We listen to:
- what is said
- the way it is said.

We observe:
- body language
- facial expressions and gestures.

Example:

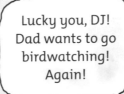

Reading between the lines, we can tell the following:
- The boys are friends.
- DJ is probably going on holidays with his family.
- DJ can swim.
- Tom thinks DJ will have a better holiday than him.
- Tom doesn't really want to go birdwatching.

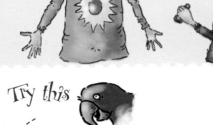

Try this

Interestingly, much of the meaning we draw from text is implied. Many signs and symbols carry implied meanings.

What meanings do you make from these signs and symbols?

3. Personal (evaluative) comprehension

It is at the **personal comprehension** level that we step back from the text and reflect on what we have read or viewed, and think about what it has meant to us. We make a personal **evaluation** of the text and often like to share our views with others. Every reading encounter influences our thinking in some way.

(See How do I make personal meaning pp. 47–49, 77–78, 85)

BARRIERS TO COMPREHENSION

There are a number of reasons why people find it difficult to make meaning from text.

These include:

- not being able to read most of the words
- not having enough prior knowledge or experience to get started
- unfamiliar subject matter
- vocabulary that is too technical
- poorly written text with an unclear meaning
- not knowing the meaning of individual words in their context
- not having a clear purpose for reading
- not understanding the purpose of the author
- not being able to understand the language used within the culture
- not being part of 'the group'.

People with similar interests tend to gather into groups. Scientists meet with other scientists, golfers with other golfers, video game enthusiasts with other video game players. Within the group, they tend to use their own **jargon**, and people outside the group are often unable to understand them.

Example:

I heard that one of the markers of the QCS Test got the tap on the shoulder last week.

Comprehending texts

TEN TIPS FOR READERS

1 Remember, **making meaning starts with you** — with what you already know, feel and believe about the topic.

2 Know WHY you are reading (or viewing) a text.

3 **Consider what the author has set out to do** — are they trying to entertain you, persuade you, instruct you or give you information?

4 Give reading (or viewing) your **full attention.** It is important to become engaged and stay engaged with what the author is saying and where the author is leading your thinking. Remember, you are the one who must make meaning from the text!

5 **Pause often** during reading and reflect on the characters, the actions, the information, the illustrations or even just the beauty of the language.

6 If you lose track of the meaning, go back and pick up the threads.

7 **Read, watch and listen!** Build your vocabulary and understanding of words and everyday expressions. The more you know, the easier it will be to make meaning from text.

8 Make your dictionary your best friend. Use it often to find the meanings of words. Add these words to your own vocabulary.

9 *Read anything and everything! This is the best way to understand how texts work, and how authors use language and images to achieve their purpose.*

10 You will know that you have understood a text if you are able to tell someone else about it.

READING 'LIKE A WRITER'

Writers:
- set down their ideas in a certain way (structure)
- link their ideas together in particular ways (cohesive ties).

TOP-LEVEL STRUCTURE

When we use **language**, we use different patterns of thinking to organise our ideas. These patterns, which occur over and over in text, are called **top-level structures**.

The most common patterns are:
- **cause and effect** — to explain what happened and why
- **compare and contrast** — to show how things are the same or how they are different
- **problem and solution** — a problem and how it is (or might be) solved
- **listing** — a simple list or a lot of points about the same thing.

These patterns are clearly seen in graphic representations. (See Comprehending visual texts pp. 10–14, 53–55, 86, 87)

Cause and effect
Things happen for a reason. Every cause results in an effect — one thing leads to the other.

Example:
Because it rained, [CAUSE] the match was cancelled. [EFFECT]
As a consequence of the cancellation, [CAUSE] the grand final had to be delayed. [EFFECT]

When we read, we need to think 'like a writer'.

To comprehend a text, readers need to understand:
1. how a text is constructed
2. how ideas are connected.

Here are some words and phrases that signal **cause and effect** relationships.

so, so that	because	as a result	consequently
due to	caused by	for this reason	therefore
thus	if	resulted in	an outcome of

Circle the cause and underline the effect in each sentence.

1. A grasshopper has strong back legs so it can leap long distances.
2. Many homes have been destroyed as a result of the recent bushfires.
3. The big drop in elephant numbers is largely due to the poaching of ivory.
4. If sand is heated to a very high temperature it will melt into glass.
5. When the earthquake struck, hundreds of homes crumbled to the ground.

Try this

Compare and contrast

When we **compare** ideas, we think about how they are the **same**.

When we **contrast** ideas, we think about how they are **different**.

Example:

The emu is the largest Australian bird and stands about two metres tall. It has a long, thin neck like the African ostrich, [COMPARING] but it is neither as big nor as heavy. [CONTRASTING] Like all birds, emus and ostriches have feathers, two legs and two wings, [COMPARING] but, unlike most birds, they cannot fly. [CONTRASTING]

Here are some words and phrases that signal **comparing and contrasting**.

Comparing		Contrasting	
like, likewise	compared with	however	unlike
similarly	in the same way	yet	but
also	both	on the other hand	whereas
just as	again	although	besides

Do the ideas in each sentence compare or contrast with each other?

1. A gum tree is an evergreen tree, whereas a jacaranda is deciduous.
2. Like all reptiles, a snake is cold-blooded and lays eggs.
3. Owls eat mice, frogs and lizards; but parrots eat seeds, nuts and plants.
4. Both oranges and lemons are used in the making of marmalade jam.
5. Unlike gold, copper will tarnish and turn green with age.

Try this

Writers can compare things by using adjectives, antonyms and their choice of vocabulary.

Examples:

- *Paul is taller than Ben.*
- *The king had great power and wealth, while his people lived in hunger and poverty.*
- *He bore a remarkable resemblance to the prince. Were they brothers?*

Problem and solution

For every **problem**, there is a real or possible **solution**.

Scientists pose problems and seek to find solutions through research and experimentation. Storywriters create problems for their characters to solve.

Examples:

Scientific
A cochlear implant is a long-term solution for people with moderate to profound hearing loss.

Story
Cinderella had nothing to wear to the ball, until her fairy godmother showed up. With a wave of her magic wand, Cinderella's fairy godmother changed Cinderella's rags into a beautiful gown. So Cinderella went off to the ball where she would meet a handsome prince.

Here are some words and phrases that signal a **problem and solution** structure.

need to prevent	problem	solution
question	answer	difficulties
outcome	in response to	as a result

Listing

Listing is a very common way of organising information. Some lists describe, some lists explain, some lists direct and some lists argue.

Lists can be vertical or horizontal, and are organised in:

Consecutive numbering (1, 2, 3, 4 ...) or bullet (dot) points also signal a list.

- a logical way — where the more obvious or important things are described first (recipes, descriptions and explanations)

- a chronological way — where events are listed in a time sequence (stories and recounts)

- simple lists — such as shopping lists or as words separated by commas. For example: *There are many kinds of pasta, including spaghetti, macaroni, fettuccine, vermicelli, tagliatelle and gnocchi.*

Here are some words and phrases that signal **listing**:

for example	also	types, kinds
such as	first, next	later
some features	for instance	to begin with
some characteristics	many parts	as time passed

COHESION

Cohesion is the way the text sticks together. Each sentence connects to the next and the ideas are linked together in a meaningful way. When a text is cohesive, the reader is able to follow the flow of meaning without difficulty.

Cohesive devices are used to tie ideas together.

COHESIVE TIES (CONNECTING IDEAS)

Cohesive ties are words or phrases used to link ideas together. These ideas are connected through the **grammar** and **vocabulary** of the text. Cohesive ties make reading flow naturally, which helps us to make sense of the whole text. We can only understand a text if it is first **coherent** (connected in a logical way).

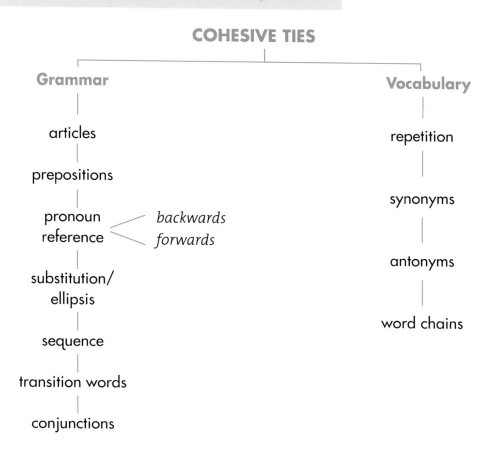

COHESIVE TIES

Grammar

articles

prepositions

pronoun reference — *backwards* / *forwards*

substitution/ ellipsis

sequence

transition words

conjunctions

Vocabulary

repetition

synonyms

antonyms

word chains

Some is the indefinite article used before plural or mass nouns.

CONNECTING IDEAS THROUGH GRAMMAR

Articles

In English, the articles **a** (or **an**) and **the** are used in front of common nouns (e.g. **a** train, **an** egg, **the** magpie).

The is **definite** about what is named. Readers and listeners can understand what it is.

Examples:
the latest fashion, the moon, the prime minister, the sixth grade

A (or **an**) is **indefinite**, indicating something readers and listeners only know in general terms.

Examples:
a fast car, an oily rag, a bus ticket, a pop star

In text, people and places are usually introduced as **a** (or **an**) then become **the** as we read on.

Example:
There was once an evil giant who lived in a tumbledown castle, deep in a dark, green forest. One day, the evil giant went riding in the forest. He returned to find the castle in flames.

Prepositions

Prepositions are words that tell us about the position of someone or something in relation to another person or thing.

Examples:
My hand could be: on the chair, above the chair, under the chair, beside the chair, over the chair, below the chair, behind the chair and on top of the chair.

A preposition introduces a **phrase** — a group of words containing a noun or pronoun but no verb.

Examples:
for Edward, to her, among the chickens, beside the door, off the table, until tomorrow

Here is a list of prepositions. They tell you where people and things are positioned.

about	before	during	off	to
above	behind	except	on	towards
across	below	for	onto	under
after	beneath	from	over	until
against	beside	in	past	up
along	between	into	since	upon
among	by	near	through	with
around	down	of	till	without

Pronoun reference

Pronouns are used in place of nouns to avoid repetition. They can refer backwards and forwards to people and things in the text. This is called **pronoun reference**.

Examples:

"Will you show me how to play chess?" Jess asked her friend, Tommy.

Jill and Adam have a pet budgie. They keep it in a cage on the verandah.

Understanding how nouns and pronouns relate to each other is important in keeping track of the meaning in text.

Substitution and ellipsis

Writers avoid cumbersome repetition by **substituting** words of the same part of speech, or leaving out words altogether by using an **ellipsis (...)**.

Examples:
I'm going to the shop to buy a chicken for dinner.
Do you want one? (chicken)
I will probably buy milk and bread too.
Do you need any? (milk and bread)
I don't know if you want potatoes, but Jeremy does.
(want some potatoes)

Sometimes, a writer uses an ellipsis to invite you to predict what might happen next.

Example:
The children heard strange noises behind the door.
"Come out! Come out!" they cried.
Out came ...

Try this

Which words have been substituted by others, or left out?
Mr Webb divided us into small groups. He explained that we would be doing a series of different maths activities. Some of them would be easier than others and points would be awarded for successfully completing each one. Each small group would move from one activity to another and attempt to complete as many as possible in one hour.

Transistion words are links in the chain of meaning.

Transition (connecting) words

Transition words and phrases connect ideas together in particular ways. They guide readers from one sentence to the next. Understanding the way ideas relate to each other is important in comprehending text.

Addition

Transition words are used to **add** information.

Examples:
Sam threw on a sweater, grabbed her camera and hurried out the door.
Jordon, as well as all his classmates, hurried to get tickets for the game.

Here are some transition words and phrases that signal added information.

and	too	again	furthermore
besides	also	together with	moreover
in addition	equally	not only … but also	as well as
first, second, third	similarly	in the same way	likewise

Time

Sequence is an important element of narratives.

Transition words and phrases place events in a **time setting**, or show the **sequence** of events.

Example:
At first, the shipwrecked men didn't know what to do. Then one of them suggested lighting a flare. Finally, they were rescued by the men on a passing trawler who had seen their distress signal.

Here are some words and phrases that signal time settings and sequence.

after	afterwards	at first	later	immediately
while	at the same time	thereafter	soon	currently
previously	in the future	at that time	in the end	finally
since (then)	shortly	so far	before	earlier
meanwhile	during	now, until now	then	in the past

Place

Transition words and phrases show the place or **location** of events.

Example:
In the distance, I could see the old, empty brick factory behind its tangled wire fence. Up on the roof, the sun glanced off a small skylight between two tall chimneys. Ivy clung to the left wall, and red bricks lay broken among the tall weeds.

Here are some words and phrases that signal place.

here, there	in the distance	up, down	under, over	alongside
in front of	between	beside	above, below	to the left/right
opposite to	behind	around	across	on this side
before, after	in the background	nearby	beyond	further
in the middle	beneath	among	adjacent to	across

Conjunctions

Conjunctions are joining words. They join ideas together in a meaningful way. **Coordinating conjunctions** join:

Words

NOUNS   *Jack and Jill; tea or coffee;*

ADJECTIVES   *tired but happy; yellow or blue*

ADVERBS   *here and there; fast or slow; quickly but carefully*

PRONOUNS   *she and I; us or them; no-one but me*

Phrases

Sue went up the steps and into the house.
They battled across the river and up the bank.

Simple sentences (compound sentences)

Jack is leaving now, but he will be back later.
Sue is going to Perth and I am going with her.
It's getting dark, so I'll walk home with you.

Conjunctions join words, phrases and sentences.

These words are **coordinating conjunctions**:

and	but	so	for	yet	or	nor

Subordinating conjunctions join **principal clauses** (main clauses) and **subordinate clauses** (dependent clauses):

Examples:
She was late because she lost her way.
I will wait until my friends arrive.
When the lights went out, we lit a candle.
I'll look after the animals while you're away.
We'll have lunch then we'll go for a walk.

These words are **subordinating conjunctions**:

after	as	although	before	once	because	then	though
therefore	until	unless	where	wherever	when	while	since

Correlative conjunctions are used in **pairs**:

Examples:
I don't know whether to go skating or to the movies.
Both Angela and Carol left early.
I will come as soon as I can.

These words are **correlative conjunctions**:

either … or	neither … nor	whether … or	not … but	not only… but also
as … as	no sooner … than	both … and	if … then	between … and

CONNECTING IDEAS THROUGH VOCABULARY

Repetition
Words are often **repeated** in a text to make meaning clear.

Example:
Basket weaving (also called basketry or basket making) is the process of weaving vegetable fibres into a basket. People who weave baskets are called basketmakers and basketweavers. Baskets are made from a variety of materials, including straw, animal hair and grasses.

Synonyms

To avoid constant repetition, and to make text more appealing, writers replace words with ones that have the same or similar meaning. These are called **synonyms**.

Examples:

glad = *joyful*

save = *rescue*

laugh = *chuckle*

runaway = *fugitive*

plain = *ordinary*

In stories, the verb 'say' can be replaced by any number of words to better show the changing moods of the characters: groan, mumble, laugh, snarl, growl, moan, whisper, scream, shout, simper.

Antonyms

Words that are opposite in meaning can also bring variety of expressions to text. These words are called **antonyms**.

Example:

It seems that employers are constantly demanding more work for less pay. Workers dislike unfairness of any kind and are demanding that justice be done. They are calling on the government to make new laws to right the wrongs.

In *A Tale of Two Cities*, Charles Dickens uses antonyms to set the colourful opening scene:

It was the best of times, it was the worst of times,

it was the age of wisdom, it was the age of foolishness ...

it was the season of Light, it was the season of Darkness,

it was the spring of hope, it was the winter of despair,

we had everything before us, we had nothing

before us ...

Word chains

In text, you will find words that 'go together'. Here are some **key words** you would expect to see if you were reading a book about bikes. These words form the thread of meaning, or 'chain', that runs through the text.

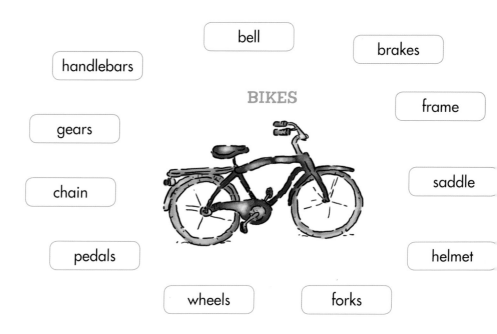

bell

brakes

handlebars

BIKES

frame

gears

saddle

chain

pedals

helmet

wheels

forks

Read this text and find the words that relate to 'clothes'.

Cycling in comfort

Clothes should be loose and comfortable. Shorts are ideal. Wear a T-shirt and take a sweater in case the weather turns cold. Underclothing is best made of cotton, as it absorbs perspiration well. Remember, you must always wear a helmet for safety. In winter, you may need gloves to keep your hands warm. Always carry something to protect you from the rain. A light raincoat is ideal. Always wear brightly coloured clothes or luminous socks so that you are clearly visible to other traffic.

Try this

FICTION

Imaginative texts are written to entertain the reader.

When we read stories, we step into a land of make-believe, with imaginary characters, settings and events.

Imaginative texts are written to entertain or amuse the reader. Authors lace their stories with rich, metaphorical language to engage the reader deeply with the characters and the action.

COMPREHENDING NARRATIVES

As language users, we have developed a whole range of strategies to help us understand what people speak and write about.

As readers, we use these same strategies, often unconsciously, to make meaning from stories of the imagination. These stories are written to entertain or amuse the reader.

All **narratives** have the same basic structure and language features.

STRUCTURE

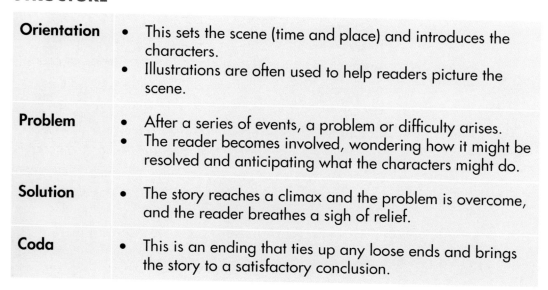

Orientation	• This sets the scene (time and place) and introduces the characters. • Illustrations are often used to help readers picture the scene.
Problem	• After a series of events, a problem or difficulty arises. • The reader becomes involved, wondering how it might be resolved and anticipating what the characters might do.
Solution	• The story reaches a climax and the problem is overcome, and the reader breathes a sigh of relief.
Coda	• This is an ending that ties up any loose ends and brings the story to a satisfactory conclusion.

FEATURES

- written in first or third person
- written in present or past tense
- doing, saying and thinking verbs
- adjectives and adverbs used to describe characters and events
- dialogue between characters
- conjunctions

Note how one event leads to another (**cause and effect**) and how a **problem** leads to a **solution**. There is often more than one problem (and solution) in a story. The author brings the story to life by **comparing and contrasting** settings, characters, feelings and actions.

(See Top-level structure pp. 23–26)

Think of a story as a big list of events happening in chronological order.

HOW DO I GET STARTED?

Get ready to read by taking a close look at the book you are about to read. It gives you information to help you get 'tuned in' to the story. It calls to mind any knowledge or past experiences you've had with this type of story. This will give you a launch pad from which the story can unfold.

STRATEGIES
Previewing
Making connections
Predicting

Previewing

The **cover** of a book is designed to attract your attention and invite you into the story.

Check out:

- **the title and cover picture**

  What do they suggest about the story?

  Will the story be interesting, exciting or funny?

  Will it be an adventure story, science-fiction, fantasy or legend?

- **the author**

  Have you read other books by this author?

  Is the book part of a set or series by this author?

  Did someone recommend this author?

- **the blurb on the back**

  What does it reveal about the story?

  Does it make you want to read more?

Browse through the pages to get a sense of the story. Remember, words and pictures work closely together to make meaning.

Ask yourself:

- Who are the characters?

- What do the pictures tell me about the characters, the setting and the storyline?

- Where and when might this story be taking place?

- Is this a picture book or a story book?

- Is the book written in chapters?

- Is the print large or small? (Generally, the larger the print, the simpler the words.)

- How long will it take me to read it?

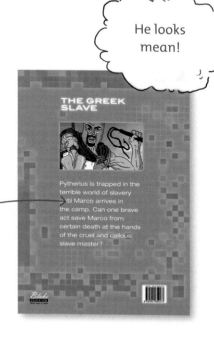

Back cover blurb

Pytherius is trapped in the terrible world of slavery until Marco arrives in the camp. Can one brave act save Marco from certain death at the hands of the callous slave master?

Making connections

As we **preview** the text, our thoughts become focused on what we already know — in this case, about Greece, slaves and soldiers. We begin **making connections** with other stories we've read or movies we've seen. The pictures show us the characters and the setting, and give us some clues as to the action that might take place.

Read the beginning of the story, but don't spoil the ending by reading the last paragraph!

Chapter One

He stood against the skyline, the warrior soldier, his helmet gleaming in the sunlight, his blood-red cloak dancing in the wind. He was as tall as his pointed spear and his eyes were as cold and hard as the sword at his belt.

This is how Pytherius first saw the man who would be his slave master. His name was Cyrus — a name that would be written on his heart forever.

Predicting

Readers usually like to guess, or **predict**, what might happen next in a story. Once they begin to read, they start to predict how the story might unfold.

From our preview of *The Greek Slave*, we can predict that this is probably a story where the 'good guy' wins. We are probably already thinking that:

- Pytherius is the 'goodie' — the hero of the story
- the slave master is the 'baddie'
- Pytherius will outsmart the slave master and save Marco.

As the action unfolds, we check to see if our predictions are true, and we continue to predict what each of the characters might do next.

> The pictures also help us with our predictions. They show us what we can expect to happen.

HOW DO I KEEP TRACK OF THE STORY?

When we read a book, the story unfolds in our imagination. Right from the very first words, we begin to make meaning at three levels — **literal**, **inferential** and **personal**. We meet the characters, then we keep track of what they are doing, how they are feeling and how they resolve any problems. (See Three levels of comprehension pp. 18–21)

STRATEGIES

Visualising   Monitoring

Making connections

Predicting   Inferring

Reflecting

Visualising

As we read, we bring the characters to life in our imagination. We **visualise** or make pictures of them in our mind. Try to place yourself 'inside' the story with the characters — watching them, seeing where they are and what they are doing. Pretend you are making a movie that clearly shows the characters, the settings and the action.

Visualising is a very powerful **strategy** for making sense of a story as it unfolds in your imagination.

Try this

Read this description of Professor Splott then close your eyes and visualise him. Now draw a quick sketch of what you think he might look like.

I was not prepared for Professor Splott. He oozed into the room like a long, brown stick insect. He was taller than I thought anyone could be and his long face was like stretched chewing gum. His bald head shone like a polished egg. He wore a white shirt with a bright yellow tie, and his grey pants were stained and wrinkled. He sidled across the room, his long, bony fingers clutching a short stick, which he slapped against his thigh. He looked at me over his wire-framed glasses, his beady brown eyes boring into my brain.
"Well, Brown, what have you done this time?" he asked in a menacing tone.

Ask yourself: Does it sound right? Does it make sense?

Remember,
the meanings of many
terms and phrases are
implied. We often need
to read between the
lines to understand
and keep track of
the meaning.

(See Metaphors p. 6 and Inferential
comprehension pp. 19–20)

Monitoring

As we read, we are constantly checking or **monitoring** that the story is making sense to us.

If you lose track of what is happening in the story, you need to:

- STOP
- GO BACK to the beginning of the sentence, paragraph or chapter
- RE-READ that section.

If you come to a word you don't know, you need to:

- READ ON past the word
- THINK about what you already know is happening
- LOOK at any pictures that might help
- LOOK at the first letter of the word and make a guess
- SOUND OUT the word as best you can
- CHECK the dictionary
- GO BACK and READ that part again.

HOW DO I KEEP TRACK OF THE CHARACTERS?

As we read, we are constantly 'connecting the dots': making connections between words, within sentences and across paragraphs to keep track of the characters and events.

Pronoun reference

In a story, the characters are introduced by name (e.g. Pytherius, Marco, Cyrus). As the story continues, they are either called by their name or referred to by a **pronoun**. We keep track of the characters by 'connecting these dots' throughout the text.

(See Pronoun reference p. 29)

Example:

"How did *you* come to be a slave, *Marco*?" *Pytherius* asks.

"*I* was kidnapped from *my* father's house two months past. *I'm* sure

Cyrus will be asking for a large sum of gold for *my* return."

"Then *I* must get *you* home, *Marco*, before *he* finds us!"

Pytherius says, *his* face serious.

Read this paragraph. Which characters do the pronouns refer to?

Pytherius steps forward. "**I** am Pytherius and this is Marco, son of Mykos, a nobleman from Athena," **he** says.
"**I** don't care who **you** are, or whose son **he** is," Lena says coldly, **her** arrow pointed at Marco. "**You** are on **my** father's land."

The names of objects are replaced by **it** (singular), **they** and **them** (plural).

Try this

Example:
The wave smashes into the boat. It lifts the boat like a leaf in the wind. It scoops up the two men and carries them, gasping and gulping towards the beach. It dumps them, then rolls on towards the sea cliffs. It swirls and boils around the scattered rocks before flowing back out to sea.

Example:
Geraldine Georgina Jones loved making models. Her room was filled with them — ships, dinosaurs, birds, trains and planes. She had carefully glued the pieces together and painted them, using fine brushes and tiny pots of paint. They were so precious to her that she wouldn't let anyone else touch them.

Sometimes, **it** (or **they**) refers to an idea rather than an object or animal.

Example:
Let's make a run for it.
They say there will be a storm this afternoon.
That's it! I've had enough.

Try this

Dialogue

Dialogue brings the characters to life and moves the story forward. We quickly understand what characters are like by what they say and how they say it. Are they friendly, bossy, calm or honest? We can also see how different characters relate to each other. Are they friends, enemies or strangers?

Read these paragraphs. What do you think each character is like and how do the characters relate to each other?

The sound of shouting reaches their ears. It is a voice Marco recognises.
"Get your back into it, you lazy slave!" Karim shouts.
Marco's face darkens with anger. "Wait here, Jago. Pytherius and I will take care of this thug!"

"Who is it, Miranda?" asks Marco. She peeps through the window.
"It's Karim," she whispers, looking frightened.
"Just the person I want to see," Marco growls. "Take Lena to her room, Miranda, and stay with her."
His father rests a hand on Marco's shoulder. "Now don't you go being a hothead, son!" Marco crosses the room and yanks open the door.

Punctuation

Punctuation marks divide text into meaningful chunks of language so that we can more easily follow the flow of written language.

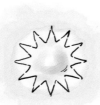

Stories are written in sentences marked by:

- **full stops** (for statements) — *The sun burns down from a clear, blue sky.*
- **question marks** (for questions) — *Stavros? Do you not recognise me?*
- **exclamation marks** (for emphasis) — *Stop everything!*

Speech marks enclose words that are spoken.

"Your plan didn't work, Karim," she says angrily.

Capital letters introduce sentences and announce the names of characters and places.

"Costos knows my father, Pytherius. He will give us horses to ride back to Athena," Marco says.

Commas within sentences:

- separate words in a list — *Thick, black, choking smoke fills the air.*
- mark beginning phrases — *By midmorning, the sun is high and a stiff wind is blowing.*
- mark embedded phrases or clauses — *No, my friend, I'm going into politics.*
- separate spoken and unspoken words — *"My messenger has brought news from Sparta," he says.*
- separate independent clauses joined by 'and' (or another conjunction) in a long sentence — *"The sun rises quickly with the promise of another hot day, and there is not a breath of wind to stir the leaves of the trees."*

If more than one idea in a list contains a conjunction, add a comma before the 'and' that introduces the last idea.

"His face is black and tear-stained, his eyes are red and swollen, and his clothes are scorched and torn."

HOW DO I KEEP TRACK OF THE EVENTS?

Time sequence
In a story, the events usually follow each other in a **time sequence**.

The passing of time in stories is indicated by words and phrases such as:

As the sun rose ...	*During that long afternoon ...*
Later that day ...	*Now ...*
At sunset ...	*In the soft moonlight ...*
Suddenly ...	*After a while ...*
Several days later ...	*Then ...*

Sometimes, an author will use **flashbacks** to tell a story. This means that part of the story is told out of sequence. For example, the author might begin with a particular event then go back and relate the events that led up to it.

Finding it hard to keep track of the meaning?
Go back a few paragraphs and scan through them to find the main ideas.
This will help you pick up the threads of the story.

Paragraphs

Authors write stories in short segments called **paragraphs**. This is very helpful to the reader because each new paragraph signals a change of time or setting, a new idea, or the beginning of another event. Each paragraph centres on a **main idea** with supporting details. Each sentence builds on the one before it. Paragraphs make it easier for the reader to keep track of what is happening.

Example:

Setting the scene
Two children discover an old house.

The old, crumbling, sandstone house rose out of the gloom. In the distance, thunder crackled and intermittent flashes of lightning lit up the falling roof and broken shutters. Two children moved cautiously towards the heavy, wooden door.

How are the children feeling? What might happen next?

Jo sees a wooden trunk through the keyhole.

Jo peered through the large keyhole. The room was bare. In the brief flashes, she saw a large, carved, wooden trunk in the middle of the room. It had a curved lid and shiny, brass latches. She felt strangely excited.
Tommy tugged her arm and whispered, "What is it? What can you see?"
"An old, wooden trunk, just as the gypsy said," answered Jo. She nudged Tommy. "C'mon, let's go take a look," she whispered.

How are the children feeling? What might happen next?

The children enter the room and touch the wooden trunk.

Hardly daring to breathe, Tommy turned the large iron knob. The door creaked slowly inwards. The children stepped inside the room cautiously. The breeze sent the cobwebs trembling. They tiptoed towards the old trunk. Jo brushed her hand over the curved lid, sending dust dancing in the air.

What might be in the trunk? What might happen next?

The door is locked and the children are trapped.

Suddenly, the door slammed shut and a key was turned in the lock. The sound echoed through the empty room. The children looked at each other in horror as footsteps faded into silence. They rushed to the door and tried to tug it open, but it wouldn't budge …

What might happen next?

Making connections

During reading, you continue to be 'inside' the story with the characters, sharing their hopes, their fears, their adventures, their dangers and triumphs. You can also be 'outside' the story — where you **make connections** between what is happening and other stories you've read, or between the characters and people you know. You'll wonder how you'd behave and what you would do in the same situation. Connecting with the story in this way makes the story personal and meaningful.

In detective stories, the author likes to keep you guessing 'whodunnit' right up to the end of the book!

Predicting

It is fun to **predict** what a character might do next, what challenges they might face and how they might overcome them.

Try this

Read these texts and predict what might happen next.

1. "Tomorrow, Costos will provide us with horses to ride back to Athena," says Marco.
"Horses!" exclaims Pytherius, wide-eyed.
Seeing the look of concern on Pytherius's face, Marco laughs. "You can't ride, can you, Pytherius?" he asks. Pytherius shakes his head.

2. The museum guard closed the glass case containing the ancient Greek urn and locked it with a small, silver key. He took one final glance around the room and turned to leave. The heavy door swung closed behind him and a key grated in the lock. He hadn't noticed the slight hitch in the curtain in a shadowy corner of the room.

Reflecting

It is important to pause during your reading to **reflect** on the story, perhaps at the end of a chapter, or after reading an exciting or thought-provoking part. This gives you breathing space to think about and savour what is happening, to think about what the characters are feeling and to predict what might happen next. If you rush through your reading, you can easily miss important details. Stopping to reflect helps you keep track of the meaning, and perhaps will lead you to go back and clarify something before reading on.

Finding it hard to keep track of the meaning?
Write some reflections on a post-it note and stick it at the end of the chapter. If you lose track of the story, go back and read your notes again.

Inferring

Many stories contain meaning that is **inferred** (or implied) rather than literal. To discover this meaning, we use bits of information from the text to come to some logical conclusion. (See Three levels of comprehension pp. 18–21)

What meanings are inferred in the following texts?

They can see a red glow in the hills beyond the olive groves. There is a smell of smoke in the air.

Conclusion: There is a bushfire in the hills.

The days grew longer. The sun grew stronger. Peter Sox stopped lighting the fire. Bobby Sox threw off her bed socks and packed away her patchwork quilt.

Conclusion: _____

Jem began to feel anxious. How was he going to survive another day without water? What if no one had seen his signal? What if a wild animal attacked him? What if…? He tried not to panic.

Conclusion: _____

Try this

Figurative language

Authors often use **figurative language** to make their stories more colourful and interesting. Meaning is inferred rather than literal. (See Comprehending words pp. 3–7)

Simile: "You'll have to run *like the wind* to beat me, Pytherius!" Marco says laughingly.

Metaphor: "Well, Marco, did you *kick up a storm* at the Assembly today?"

Personification: A storm builds suddenly, *born of the oppressive heat* that has been simmering all day. *Lightning tears at the clouds* until they burst.

HOW DO I MAKE PERSONAL MEANING?

When we come to the end of a story, we usually stop and think about the events, the characters, and our own thoughts and feelings. We think about what the story meant to us personally, what we might have learned, what might have touched our hearts and what memories we might take away.

STRATEGIES
Reflecting
Retelling
Summarising
Responding

Reflecting

When we think back over the story, we usually make judgements about the storyline, the characters and the events. We give the story our own personal rating, somewhere between just okay and amazing, while another reader may give it a different rating.

We might, for example, **reflect** on:

- *what we liked or didn't like*
- *whether the characters were believable*
- *whether the story was exciting, funny or scary*
- *whether the story had a satisfactory ending*
- *whether there were loose ends*
- *whether we liked the language used*
- *whether the illustrations added meaning to the words*
- *whether we learned any new words*
- *what we might have done if faced with the same situations as the characters.*

Retelling

We often like to tell others about our reading experiences, especially after reading a great story. When you retell a story, focus on the main characters and events, and the problem and resolution.

Here is an idea to help you with your **retelling**:

Setting
Characters
Events
Problem
Book title
Author
Solution

Don't spoil the story for someone else by telling them what happens in the end!

Summarising

Write a **summary** to capture the story. Write only about the main events. Keep it short and don't get tied up in dialogue and detail. Browse back through any book illustrations — they usually capture the main events. You might also like to add your personal judgement of the story. Write your summary as a diary entry or book review.

Cinderella

Cinderella lived with her stepsisters in an old castle. She was made to work in the kitchen. One day there was to be a great ball. Everyone was invited, but Cinderella was not allowed to go. A fairy godmother appeared and, with the help of her magic wand, she dressed Cinderella in a beautiful gown and sent her off to the ball in a grand coach. The prince danced with her until, at midnight, Cinderella fled down the stairs, losing one glass slipper. The prince searched everywhere until he found his Cinderella. They were married and lived happily ever after.

Responding

You **respond** to a story by capturing your thoughts and feelings about it. There are many ways you can do this. Here are some suggestions:

- *Make a timeline of events in the story.*
- *Write an autobiography of a character in the book.*
- *Write an advertisement for the book.*
- *Make a mask of a character in the book.*
- *Take on the role of a character and answer questions about yourself.*
- *Draw a portrait of a favourite character.*
- *Prepare a version of the story to read aloud to young children.*
- *Prepare a little book of interesting words and quotes from the story.*
- *Write a diary for your favourite character.*
- *Make a map of the setting of the story.*

A WORD ABOUT PLAYS

A **play** is a story that is written to be performed onstage by **actors**. The story is told through the dialogue, movements, gestures and facial expressions of the characters (actors). The actors may wear **costumes** and perform onstage against painted **scenery** (backdrops), while stage **props** are used to create the **setting**. Props include things such as chairs, lamps, baskets, books, telephones, tables and potted plants.

If you are reading a **play script**, you make meaning from the characters' words and the stage directions, which are written in italics. If you are viewing a play, you make meaning by listening to what the actors are saying and watching what they are doing. Like all stories, a play has an underlying problem and solution structure.

Example:
(The sound of knocking on a door, stage left. Marco crosses to the door and yanks it open.)

MARCO: So Karim, you dare show your face here?

KARIM: You have something that belongs to me! *(shouting)*

MARCO: Do I? And what might that be?

KARIM: That girl from Sparta.

A WORD ABOUT MOVIES

Movies are also dramatic performances and begin with a **movie script**. Movies are **multimodal texts**, so we must make meaning from the audio and visual elements at the same time.

The characters may be real people or animated figures. Throughout the story, the characters are filmed in settings that are real, or constructed in a movie studio. Movie directors use a range of techniques to present the story in a particular way. We make meaning as the story unfolds, so we must give it our full attention.

Unlike a book — where we can stop, reflect and re-read — we can't pause or replay a scene (unless we are watching a DVD).

As we view a movie, we make meaning from:

- **movement**
- **dialogue** and **voice** (pitch, volume, emphasis, speed of delivery)
- **gestures, facial expressions** and **body language**
- **costumes** — including wigs and makeup
- **lighting** — to depict time of day and to create different moods
- **different camera angles** — to give viewers different experiences of a subject
- **music** — to create a particular mood (scary, exciting, sad, joyful)
- **sound effects** — to make things 'real' (door slamming, phone ringing, screaming)
- **fade-ins** (to a new scene) — to signal a change of time or setting.

A WORD ABOUT POETRY

Poetry is easily recognised by the way it looks on the page.

What is time
But the tick of a clock
The sweep of the tide
And windmills turning
Passing storms
And fading rainbows
Ripples in sand
And the summer wind dying

Rhythm is the
essential element of
poetry!

Poetry has several characteristics:

SHAPE	The way the poem 'looks' on the page
FORM	The way the poem is put together (cinquain, quatrain, haiku, acrostic, sonnet, blank verse)
RHYME	Some poems have rhyming lines and some don't. Those that do can have different patterns (AABB ABAB ABCA ABBA).
RHYTHM	All poems have a regular pulse or 'heartbeat' — some fast, some slow.
CONTENT	What the poem is about (stories, events, everyday things, thoughts and emotions)

(See *Blake's Writer's Guide* for more details about poetry.)

NON-FICTION TEXTS

Non-fiction texts often contain facts and supply information.

Non-fiction texts can be divided into two broad categories — information texts and persuasive texts. Each category contains a range of different text types.

INFORMATION TEXTS

Reports

science reports

biographies

documentaries

news reports

Procedures

recipes

directions

instructions

experiments

Recounts

letters

diaries/journals

autobiographies

factual recounts

Explanations

manuals

handbooks

how and why texts

life cycles

PERSUASIVE TEXTS

Expositions

one-sided arguments

letters to the editor

advertisements

Discussions

two-sided arguments

debates

book/TV reviews

Not all texts look the same or are structured the same way. Here are some general questions to ask yourself when reading non-fiction texts:

- Why was the text written?
- What do I want to know?
- What does the text 'look like'?
- How does the text 'work'?
- How do the visuals 'work'?
- How do the ideas in the text relate to each other?

(See *Blake's Writer's Guide* for detailed descriptions of the structures and features of non-fiction texts.)

HOW DO VISUALS HELP ME?

Information texts usually include photos (with **captions**), pictures, **graphs**, **labelled diagrams**, **flow charts** and so on. They represent shortcuts to meaning.

Through these **visuals**, you can:

- clarify and extend your understanding of the written text
- visualise and memorise information
- build knowledge and vocabulary
- summarise the information.

Here are some examples:

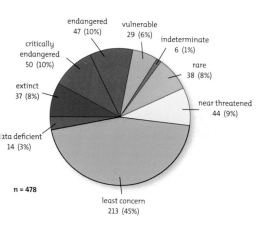

Pie chart reporting on
endangered animals
Structure: Comparing

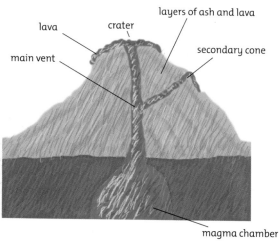

Cross section explaining
how a volcano occurs
Structure: Cause and effect

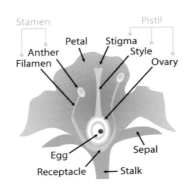

Cutaway showing
parts of a flower
Structure: Listing

The koala belongs to a
special group of mammals
called marsupials.

Photo and **caption**
reporting on koalas
Structure: Listing

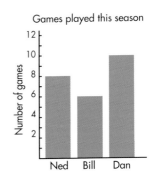

Games played this season

Bar graph reporting
on school sport
Structure: Comparing

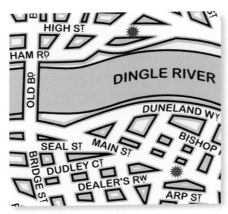

BEGIN
1. Drive north-west on Main St.
2. Turn left onto Seal St.
3. Drive west on Seal St.
4. Turn right onto Bridge St.
5. Continue north onto Old Bd. and over the Dingle River.
6. Turn right onto High St.
7. Continue driving east until you reach your destination.
END

Street map
showing directions
Structure: Listing

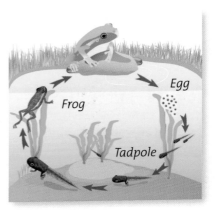

Flow chart explaining the
life cycle of a frog
Structure: Cause and effect

		The top ten boys' names in Australia in 2014 and the change from 2013	
1	Harry	6893	no change
2	Oliver	6324	no change
3	Jack	5933	no change
4	Charlie	5302	no change
5	Jacob	4905	up three
6	Thomas	4677	no change
7	Lachlan	4562	down two
8	Riley	4497	up five
9	William	4363	up one
10	James	4305	down three

Table listing data comparing
favourite names in 2014 and 2013
Structure: Listing

WHALES — have hair, live birth, breathe air

live in water, have fins, can swim

FISH — lay eggs, have scales, breathe water

Venn diagram comparing and
contrasting whales and fish
Structure: Compare and contrast

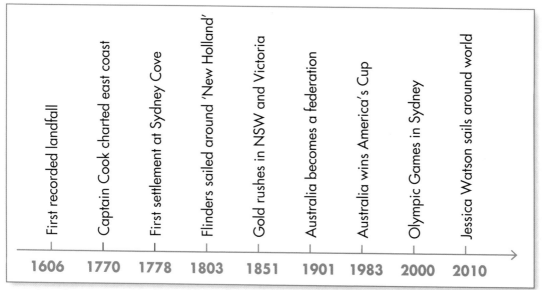

Timeline listing significant events in Australia's history *Structure: Listing*

FACT OR OPINION?

When you read non-fiction texts, it is important to know whether the author is stating **facts** or just voicing an **opinion**. Facts are true statements about a topic and can be proven. Opinions are what someone thinks about a topic. Someone else may think differently.

Try this

Examples:
The Great Barrier Reef lies off the east coast of North Queensland. [FACT]
It is the most beautiful marine park in the world [OPINION] and is a perfect tourist destination. [OPINION]

The Holden Company was founded in 1856 as a saddlery manufacturer. [FACT]
It began manufacturing car upholstery in 1908 [FACT] and produced the first all-Australian car in 1948. [FACT]
Holden produced cars that were faster and more economical than other companies. [OPINION]
Most Australians favoured Holden over all other brands. [OPINION]
Today, Holden has to compete in the global market against cheaper, foreign-made cars. [FACT]

Read each statement. Is it a fact or an opinion?

1. Mount Everest is the highest mountain in the world.
2. Ned Kelly was born in Victoria in 1855, the son of Irish parents.
3. A koala is a cuddly Australian bear.
4. Man first walked on the Moon in 1969.
5. Diamonds are a girl's best friend.

COMPREHENDING INFORMATION TEXTS

Information comes in many forms and from many sources. It can be spoken, written or visual. Most written information is supported by visuals such as photos, maps, diagrams, graphs and so on.

Writers design their texts to help the reader by:
- grouping information *(headings, subheadings)*
- highlighting information *(colours, capital letters, bold type, italics)*
- connecting information *(arrows, numbered or dot point lists)*
- organising information *(columns, paragraphs, lists, tables)*
- cross referencing *(asterisks, footnotes)*.

In the school setting, we usually find the information we need in books or short articles, or on websites.

First, you need to know what you want information about and how you want to use it. For example, you may have to write a report on the solar system, ants or the Olympic Games, or explain to the class where rain comes from or the life cycle of a bee. You may want to make origami flowers or construct a model of an energy-efficient house, or you might simply be interested in (or curious about) the topic. Once you have located the resource you need, it's time to get started.

HOW DO I GET STARTED?

STRATEGIES
Skimming and scanning
Making connections
Predicting

Skimming and scanning

Skimming and scanning are valuable tools to help you to extract information from a text quickly. **Skimming** involves running your eyes quickly over the text to get an idea of what the text is about. **Scanning** involves looking for specific bits of information — dates, names, key words and so on. You might scan through a sporting list to find your name, through the telephone book to find a plumber or through a TV guide to find a particular program.

Title

Contents

Glossary

Index

Making connections

Begin by reading the **title** (e.g. *Australian Animals, Airships and Hot Air Balloons, Keeping Your Body Healthy, Dinosaurs*). This is usually the BIG main idea and will help you start to **make connections** with what you already know about the topic. Gather further information from the back cover blurb and any pictures or photos.

Scan through the **contents** page. The contents page shows you what information is covered and allows you to zero in on a particular topic.

Skim through the **glossary**. This is a list of important words and their meanings, usually found at the back of the book. This list is also in alphabetical order. Again, this information helps you focus on what you may already know and what you will find out during your reading. The words in a glossary often appear in bold type in the text. You can refer back to the glossary any time during your reading.

Scan the **index** for a more detailed list of the contents of the book. This list is at the back of the book and is in alphabetical order, so information is very easy to find.

Back cover

When you have located the information you need, scan through the chapter or article. Look for headings or subheadings, dates, proper names, and words in italics or bold type. Look at any photos, captions, pictures or diagrams. Continue to **make connections** with what you already know. Remember, the more knowledge you have about a topic, the easier the text will be to understand.

Predicting

Read the first sentence of each paragraph. Thinking about what you already know, **predict** what the text is about.

Now go back and read the whole article or chapter.

HOW DO I FIND THE MAIN IDEAS?

Paragraphs

The first BIG **main idea** is the **title** of the book or article.

Most authors write in short segments of text called **paragraphs**. In an information text, a paragraph is constructed around one main idea. The clue is usually in the first sentence, often called the **topic sentence**. What follows are **details** that give added information about the topic.

Example:

Topic sentence →

The BIG main idea

Main idea →

What is a Leap Year?

Details — *A year has 365 days...or does it?* There are, in fact, 365 days, 5 hours, 48 minutes and 46 seconds in a year. This is a solar year, the time taken for the Earth to revolve around the Sun. It was the ancient Egyptians who first discovered that the solar year and the man-made calendar year did not always match.

A year has more than 365 days.

↓

Details — *The time accumulated every year is approximately a quarter of a day.* For centuries, an extra day was added to the calendar every four years. This kept the calendar in tune with the seasons. This extra day was called a leap day. It was the Romans who first marked February 29 as leap day.

↓

Every fourth year has an extra day.

↓

Details — *In the 16th century, calculating leap day became more precise.* The extra day was added only to those years divisible by four. That means 2016, 2020 and 2024 will be leap years. Century years (those marking the beginning of a new century) only include a leap day if exactly divisible by 400. Thus 1900 was not a leap year, but 2000 was.

↓

Calculating leap days became more exact.

↓

Details — *Babies born on February 29 are leap day babies.* Birthdays are celebrated in non-leap years on either February 28 or March 1. If you were born on a leap day, you would be over eighty years old before you could celebrate your 'official' twenty-first birthday.

↓

Leap day babies have different birthdays.

Which statement best expresses the main idea of this paragraph?

The careless dumping of rubbish can cause pollution. Flies breeding in rotting rubbish can spread disease. Animals may become sick from eating it or be hurt by sharp objects, wire and broken glass. Poisons used by farmers to control weeds and pests, as well as fertilisers used to boost plant growth, can pollute the soil. Animals eating grass grown on poisoned land can become sick. Toxins can be passed through the food chain and may affect people's health.

1. Farmers use poisons to control pests and weeds.
2. Animals get sick eating rubbish.
3. Waste materials can contaminate the soil.

Try this

Sometimes, the main idea is in the last sentence of a paragraph.

Examples:

Why are grasshoppers green and polar bears white? The green colouring of grasshoppers makes them hard to see among the green leaves, while the white coat of the polar bear matches the colour of ice and snow. Many forest animals have spots or stripes, which help them blend in with their surroundings. This is nature's way of protecting animals against their enemies.

Many people think it is unlucky to walk under a ladder, break a mirror or open an umbrella inside a house. Friday the 13th is considered an unlucky day. On the other hand, a horseshoe, a rabbit's foot or a four-leaf clover are all signs of good luck. People who believe these things are said to be superstitious.

Main ideas help you to focus on the important parts, to summarise and to remember information.

REPORTS

Reports give factual information about a broad range of natural and man-made phenomena.

Reports give factual information about a range of subjects.

All **reports** have the same basic structure and language features.

STRUCTURE

General statement	This places the subject of the report into a category. • *A kangaroo is an Australian animal.* • *The Nile is the longest river in the world.* • *The didgeridoo is a wind instrument developed by the Indigenous people of northern Australia.*
Listing (describing)	A series of paragraphs follow that describe different aspects of the topic.

FEATURES

- written in present tense
- written in third person
- doing and being verbs
- technical vocabulary
- may contain headings and subheadings
- pictures, photos, tables and diagrams support the facts

STRATEGIES
Analysing
Finding main ideas
Making connections
Relating ideas

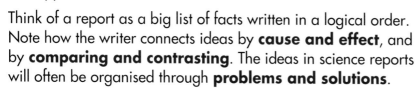

Think of a report as a big list of facts written in a logical order. Note how the writer connects ideas by **cause and effect**, and by **comparing and contrasting**. The ideas in science reports will often be organised through **problems and solutions**.

(See Top-level structure pp. 23–26)

As you read, you are constantly gathering new knowledge and **making connections** with what you already know. Keep your purpose in mind. Make **predictions**. Read the words and study the visuals — they work together to make meaning. Remember that the author is presenting a particular point of view.

HOW DOES A REPORT 'WORK'?

We can analyse a text to see how it is structured and how the author has connected the pieces of information together.

Example:

Icebergs

General statement

Comparing

Cause and effect

Icebergs are large, floating masses of ice. They form when a glacier reaches the sea and huge chunks of ice break off and float away. Large icebergs can be as tall as a fifty-storey building and several kilometres wide. Icebergs gradually melt as they float into warmer waters.

Cause and effect

Icebergs are a great danger to shipping because only a small part of the iceberg is visible above the surface of the sea. Most of it lies beneath the water and can spread out into a great shelf of ice.

Cause and effect

Ships that come too close to an iceberg risk running aground.

Problem

The Titanic, the largest and most modern passenger ship of its time, hit an iceberg in the cold waters of the Atlantic Ocean around midnight on 15 April 1912. It was one of the

Cause and effect

worst shipwrecks in history, with over 1500 lives lost. This disaster led to the establishment of an

Solution

International Ice Patrol to report on icebergs in the Atlantic shipping lanes.

glacier: a slow-moving river of ice

Listing

Example:

The BIG main idea

Topic sentence

The Emu

Main ideas

Details

The emu is a large Australian bird that stands about two metres tall. It has a long, thin neck like the African ostrich, but it is neither as big nor as heavy. Like all birds, emus and ostriches have feathers, two legs and two wings. However, unlike most birds, they cannot fly.

The emu, like the ostrich, is a large bird that cannot fly.

Details

Like the ostrich, the emu has strong, powerful legs, so it can run very fast. Speeds of over 50 kilometres an hour have been recorded.

Emus can run very fast.

Details

Emus eat berries, wild fruits, caterpillars and grass. In fact, they will eat almost anything. They can go for long periods without water, but when they find water they drink vast amounts.

Emus have a varied diet.

Details

Each year, the female lays between seven and twenty eggs in a nest on the ground. The nest is made of leaves and grass. The eggs are large and greenish-black in colour. The male emu sits on the eggs for up to eight weeks until they hatch. The chicks are striped brown and white, so they are camouflaged (well hidden) in the grass around them. By six months old they begin to look like adult birds. Emus can live for up to twenty years.

A female emu can have up to 20 chicks.

Details

Emus have good eyesight and hearing, so they are able to detect predators — such as dingoes, eagles and hawks — and keep themselves safe. They defend themselves with their strong, clawed feet by kicking, jumping, running and swerving. They are also good swimmers.

Emus are able to protect themselves.

VOCABULARY

Information reports contain **technical vocabulary** — specific words that relate to the topic. Sometimes, the writer will show the more difficult words in bold type and give you their meanings at the end of the text in a **glossary** or word bank. Sometimes the writer will suggest the meaning of a word by using brackets or dashes.

Examples:

- *The chicks are striped brown and white, so they are camouflaged (well hidden) in the grass around them.*
- *Emus have good eyesight and hearing so they are able to detect predators — such as dingoes, eagles and hawks — and keep themselves safe.*

Use a dictionary to find the meanings of any words you don't know.

HOW DO THE IDEAS RELATE TO EACH OTHER?

Reports contain ideas that relate to each other in certain ways — particularly **cause and effect**, **comparing and contrasting**, and in simple **lists** joined by commas. Look for the words that signal these relationships.
(See Top-level structures pp. 23–26, Transition (connecting) words pp. 30–31 and Conjunctions p. 31)

Example:

The Emu

The emu is a large Australian bird that stands about two metres tall. It has a long, thin neck like the African ostrich [COMPARING], but it is neither as big nor as heavy. [CONTRASTING] Like all birds, emus and ostriches have feathers, two legs and two wings. [COMPARING] However, unlike most birds, they cannot fly. [CONTRASTING]

Like the ostrich, [COMPARING] the emu has strong, powerful legs, [CAUSE] so it can run very fast. [EFFECT] Speeds of over 50 kilometres an hour have been recorded.

Like the ostrich, the emu is a large and flightless bird.

Emus eat berries, wild fruits, caterpillars and grass. [LIST] In fact, they will eat almost anything. They can go for long periods without water, but when they find water [CAUSE] they drink vast amounts. [EFFECT]

Each year, the female lays between seven and twenty eggs in a nest on the ground. The nest is made of leaves and grass. The eggs are large and greenish-black in colour. The male emu sits on the eggs [CAUSE] for up to eight weeks until they hatch. [EFFECT] The chicks are striped brown and white [CAUSE], so they are camouflaged (well hidden) [EFFECT] in the grass around them. By six months old they begin to look like adult birds. [COMPARING] Emus can live for up to twenty years.

Emus have good eyesight and hearing, [CAUSE] so they are able to detect predators [EFFECT] — such as dingoes, eagles and hawks — and keep themselves safe. They defend themselves with their strong, clawed feet, [LIST] by kicking, jumping, running and swerving. [LIST] They are also good swimmers.

The ostrich is a native bird of Africa.

As we read a report and study the visuals, we make meaning at three levels: **literal, inferential** and **personal**.

Check your understanding

Literal

* How is an emu similar or different to an ostrich?

* How does an emu defend itself?

Right there on the page

Inferential

* Why don't emus nest in trees?

* Why does the male emu sit on the eggs?

Reading between the lines

Personal

* Why might emus be a problem to farmers?

* Why do you think the emu is a protected bird?

Thinking about things

Recounts talk about the past and can be factual or personal.

RECOUNTS

Recounts tell us about past events in chronological order. They can be factual, such as historical accounts or news articles. They can also be personal, such as when people recount the everyday happenings of their lives.

All **recounts** have the same basic structure and language features.

STRUCTURE

Orientation	This sets the scene for the recount (people involved, place and time).
Events	A series of paragraphs follow that describe different events in chronological order.
Evaluation	This is where the author may comment on the events.

FEATURES

- written in past tense
- written in first or third person
- adverbs and adverbial phrases to show time and place
- technical vocabulary (in factual recounts)
- everyday vocabulary (in personal recounts)

HOW DOES A RECOUNT 'WORK'?

Read this **factual recount**. As you read, note how the events follow each other, just like a story. Think about how the writer presents the ideas and connects them together. Check the meanings of any words you don't know. Study the photos and captions, and think about what the visuals are telling you.

Think of a recount as a big list of events written in chronological order. Note how the writer connects their ideas through cause and effect, and by comparing and contrasting.
(See Top-level structure pp. 23–26)

Pompeii with Mt Vesuvius in the background

Pompeii

In the year 79 AD, Pompeii was a thriving city on the shores of the Bay of Naples in Italy. Many of its 20 000 people were rich and the town was prosperous. The streets were paved with stone. There were temples, theatres, public baths, a great amphitheatre and a covered marketplace. A wall with eight gateways surrounded the city. The city lay just over a kilometre from the foot of the volcano, Vesuvius. — Paragraph 1

On 14 August, Vesuvius began to erupt and pellets of pumice rained down on the city. Soon the streets were deep in pumice stones. People tried to escape, and at least 18 000 got away. — Paragraph 2

After several hours, the rain of pumice stopped and a rain of fine, volcanic ash began. It lasted for three days, leaving the city completely buried and many people dead. Pompeii then lay undisturbed for hundreds of years. — Paragraph 3

Traces of Pompeii were found by workmen in 1599, but careful excavation only began in 1748. Little by little, the city was unearthed. Today, thousands of tourists can walk along the pathways of this ancient city. The roofs of the buildings are gone, but parts of some walls are still standing. Ovens, cooking pots, mosaics, and bronze and marble statues help to tell the story of the people who once lived there. — Paragraph 4

The destruction of Pompeii is one of the great tragedies of history.

AD (Anno Domini): *after the birth of Christ*
pumice: *light, volcanic stone*
mosaics: *pictures made of small pieces of different coloured stones*

Read the recount about Pompeii and identify the main idea of each paragraph.

Paragraph 1
1. Pompeii had a wall with eight gateways.
2. Pompeii was a thriving city close to Mt Vesuvius.
3. Pompeii was very close to a volcano.

Paragraph 2
1. Vesuvius erupted, raining pumice stones down on the city.
2. People tried to escape from the volcano.
3. Pumice rained down on Pompeii.

Paragraph 3
1. It rained ash for three days.
2. Pompeii was buried for a long time.
3. The ash buried the city and many of its people.

Paragraph 4
1. Workmen discovered Pompeii in the 1500s.
2. People can visit the now-excavated city.
3. There are lots of statues and mosaics in Pompeii.

Try this

Read the recount about Pompeii and think about how these ideas are connected.
Example: People tried to escape [CAUSE] at least 1800 got away [EFFECT]

1. Vesuvius began to erupt [......] pellets of pumice rained down on the city [......]

2. A rain of fine, volcanic ash began [......] leaving the city completely buried [......]

3. The city was unearthed [......] thousands of tourists can walk along the pathways [......]

Dog mosaic on the floor of an ancient Roman home in Pompeii

Show the dates of these events on the timeline.

| Mt Vesuvius erupts | Pompeii buried | Traces of city found | Excavation begins | Tourists visit ruins |

2014

Try this

The great amphitheatre at Pompeii — the scene of plays and sporting events

CHECK YOUR UNDERSTANDING

Literal

* Where was Pompeii?
* What were some items that were unearthed during excavation?

  Right there on the page

Inferential

* What is the *foot* of the volcano?
* About how many people died in the eruption?

  Reading between the lines

Personal

* How can pots, mosaics and statues 'tell a story'?
* Why do you think a wall surrounded Pompeii?

  Thinking about things

Procedures list the steps to follow to acheive a goal.

PROCEDURES

Procedures show us how to make or do things by following a list of steps to achieve a goal. They are usually short and concise, leaving out unimportant words. The key to understanding a procedure is in following the steps carefully and studying any photos or diagrams.

All **procedures** have the same basic structure and language features.

STRUCTURE

Title	This clearly states the goal of the procedure *(Chocolate Crackles, How to Make a Paper Lantern)*.
List	This names the ingredients or materials required.
Method	This is a series of steps to follow to achieve the goal.

FEATURES

- written in the present tense
- each step begins with an **imperative verb** — order or command
- written in second person — speaks directly to the reader
- adjectives clarify specific steps *(beat the eggs until light and fluffy)*
- adverbs and adverbial phrases show time and place *(in the oven, next)*
- technical vocabulary
- abbreviations *(tsp. = teaspoon, g = gram)*

HOW DOES A PROCEDURE 'WORK'?

A recipe is a type of procedure. As you read the recipe below, note how it is made up of two short lists:
1. a list of materials and equipment required *(the ingredients)*
2. a list of steps to follow *(the method).*

Note how each step in the method starts with an imperative verb and what the verb is telling you to do. Think about why it is important to follow each step in a particular order when completing a procedure, and how the picture might help you.

Chocolate Crackles

Ingredients:
4 cups Rice Bubbles
½ cup icing sugar
3 tbsp. cocoa
1 cup shredded coconut
250 g copha
12 patty cases

Method:
1. **Place** the copha in a saucepan and heat gently until melted.
2. **Combine** the Rice Bubbles, sugar, cocoa and coconut in a large bowl.
3. **Add** the melted copha and mix well.
4. **Spoon** the mixture into the patty cases.
5. **Place** in the refrigerator for 1 hour to set.

copha: a type of vegetable fat made from coconut

CHECK YOUR UNDERSTANDING

Literal
* What is the main ingredient?
* What is *copha*?

Right there on the page

Inferential
* Why would you melt the copha?
* What does *tbsp.* mean?

Reading between the lines

Personal
* When would you serve chocolate crackles?
* Is this a 'healthy' food? Give reasons for your answer.

Thinking about things

Procedures are often accompanied by **diagrams** so that the reader can better **visualise** what to do.

Example:

How to Make a Paper Hat

1 Start with a rectangular piece of paper.

2 Fold the rectangle in half.

3 Fold the top corners into the middle.

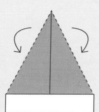

4 Take the bottom edge and fold upwards.

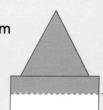

5 Turn the paper over and fold the other edge upwards.

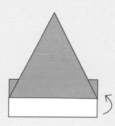

6 Open out your hat. Enjoy!

Many step-by-step procedures are available to view on the internet.

Here is a procedure for carrying out a simple science experiment. Number the steps in the correct order then predict what you think might happen. Check your prediction against the answer below.

The Power of Peas

You will need:

- a small glass jar with a lid

- a packet of dried peas

- water

- a plastic bucket

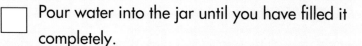

Instructions:

☐ Screw the lid on tightly.

☐ Pour water into the jar until you have filled it completely.

☐ Tap the jar lightly to settle the seeds snugly.

☐ Place the jar in a bucket and leave overnight.

☐ Fill the jar with dried peas or beans.

☐ Add more seeds until the jar is full.

Try this

Answer: The jar will break because the seeds absorb the water and expand. The pressure builds, causing the glass jar to break.

Explanations tell us how and why things work or happen.

EXPLANATIONS

Explanations tell us how and why things work or happen. They tell us about the natural world and the world of man-made things. They are often found within other texts.

All **explanations** have the same basic structure and language features.

STRUCTURE

Title	This is often a question that the text will answer. (*Why do birds migrate in winter? How does a clock work? What is a rainbow?*)
General statement	This introduces the topic.
Series of events or steps	Each paragraph contains an event or step in a process. The paragraphs are written in a logical sequence.

FEATURES

- written in present tense
- written in third person
- verbs that show action
- technical vocabulary
- conjunctions to link and sequence events
- often accompanied by flow charts and labelled diagrams

Think of an explanation as a big list of events or processes written in a logical order. It is a **causal list**, where one event or process leads to another as in **cause and effect**.
(See Top-level structure pp. 23–26)

HOW DOES AN EXPLANATION 'WORK'?

Explanations show how one process or event leads to another. These are **cause and effect** relationships and often point out the **main ideas**.

Read this explanation, noting how each paragraph presents a step in a process. Each step is clearly marked by a heading and supported by visual information. Think about how the writer connects the ideas together.

The Life Cycle of a Butterfly

General statement
↙

The butterfly is a flying insect, well known for the beautiful and colourful patterns on its wings. Like all insects, it has six legs, three body parts, and feelers or antennae. Unlike any other insect, it has scales on its wings, which lap over each other like roof tiles.

There are four different stages in the life of every butterfly.

Egg stage
1 A female butterfly lays many eggs on leaves, bark or flower heads. There is a yolk inside each egg that feeds the developing butterfly larva (caterpillar). In one to three weeks, the caterpillar is ready to hatch.

Caterpillar stage
2 The caterpillar eats its way out of the egg and begins to live on leaves and plants. It eats and eats, and it grows very fast. It grows so fast that it grows out of its skin several times. A caterpillar's new skin may be a different colour to its old skin.

Pupa stage
3 When the caterpillar is fully grown, it enters the pupa (or 'resting') stage. The insect does not move around or eat. The pupa (or chrysalis) hangs upside down from a branch, hidden among leaves, or is buried underground. It is during this stage that big changes are happening inside the pupa. Special cells that were present in the caterpillar are growing rapidly to become the legs, eyes, wings and other parts of the adult butterfly. This stage may last from a few weeks to several months.

Adult stage
4 The adult insect emerges from the pupa as a beautiful butterfly. Unlike the caterpillar — which has stubby legs, a few eyes and short antennae — the butterfly has many eyes, long legs and long antennae. It is during this stage that the female butterfly lays her eggs and the process starts all over again. Most butterflies do not eat at all and live for only one or two weeks.

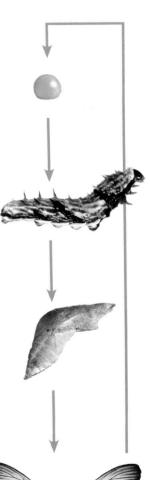

Read the text and think about how these ideas are connected. *Example:* Like all insects [COMPARING] it has six legs, three body parts, and feelers or antennae.

Try this

1. Unlike any other insect [......] it has scales on its wings.
2. It grows so fast [......] that it grows out of its skin several times. [......]
3. Unlike the caterpillar [......] the butterfly has many eyes, long legs and long antennae.
4. The female butterfly lays her eggs [......] the process starts all over again. [......]

CHECK YOUR UNDERSTANDING

Literal

- How is a butterfly different from other insects?
- What happens in the pupa stage?

Right there on the page

Inferential

- Where would you find *bark*?
- How does a caterpillar hatch?

Reading between the lines

Personal

- Is it cruel to collect butterflies? Give reasons.
- Why might caterpillars be a problem to people?

Thinking about things

Read the text, study the flow chart and answer the questions to find the main ideas.

What is the Water Cycle?

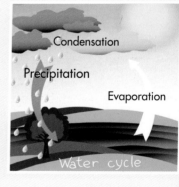
Condensation
Precipitation
Evaporation
Water cycle

Fresh water is one of our most precious resources. It falls as rain from clouds that form in the sky.

Clouds are formed through **evaporation**. When the water in the seas, lakes and dams is heated by the sun, it turns to steam or vapour. Warm air carries this vapour up into the sky. The vapour gets colder and changes back into water droplets, forming clouds. This change is called **condensation**. These tiny droplets of water join together to make bigger and bigger drops. Finally, they fall from the cloud as drops of rain (**precipitation**).

Some raindrops go into the soil. Others join together and flow along streams and rivers back to seas and lakes (**run-off**). When the sun shines, the process starts all over again. This is known as the **evaporation cycle** or **water cycle**.

1. What causes **evaporation**?
2. What causes **condensation**?
3. What causes **precipitation**?

HOW DO I MAKE PERSONAL MEANING?

We read information texts for many reasons: to catch up on news, to find out specific information, to learn how to make or do something, to understand things more deeply, or to learn about something entirely new. There is so much information available to us, especially on the internet, so we must learn to analyse and evaluate what we read.

Questioning

Here are some questions that will help you think about a text and what it has meant to you personally:

- What was the author's point of view?
- Did I find out what I wanted to know?
- Would I like to learn more about this?
- What was fact and what was opinion?
- What have I learned?
- Will this information make me think or behave differently?
- What will I do with this information (make, write or do something)?

Reviewing

You can quickly **review** a text by scanning or skimming parts of the text to find particular bits of information you'd like to remember or clarify. This also helps you find answers to questions you may be asked about the topic.

(See Skimming and scanning p. 56)

Summarising

A **summary** briefly states the main ideas and relevant details of a text. Who, what, when, where and why are helpful questions to ask yourself when writing a summary. Use any diagrams, photos or flow charts to help you, or draw your own.

A **visual summary** of the water cycle text might look like this:

A **written summary** of the water cycle text might read like this:

Water falls as rain from clouds. It soaks into the ground or flows back to the sea. The sun heats the water and it changes to vapour, which rises and forms clouds. As the water cools, it condenses into water droplets and falls as rain.

COMPREHENDING PERSUASIVE TEXTS

Persuasive texts are designed to make you think about something: to persuade you to take the writer's point of view, to buy a product or service, or to take action on a particular issue (e.g. global warming, smoking, culling sharks, fashion, junk food, littering, video games).

Persuasive texts are found in all forms of advertising, brochures, and in newspaper and magazine articles. Readers need to be aware that the text will often present the writer's opinions rather than hard facts.

HOW DO I GET STARTED?

Begin by **skimming** through the text and any visuals to find the writer's point of view. This may be in the form of a question or a statement:

Speed is the number one killer on our roads.

Looking for that perfect holiday?

Aussies are nothing but a bunch of whingers!

After hours at school, why should kids be subjected to hours of homework at night?

Think about your own point of view. **Make connections** to other texts you've read and viewed, or other opinions you've heard. Ask yourself questions such as:

- Do I agree with the writer's point of view?
- Would others think the same way?
- Is the writer stating a *fact* or an *opinion*?
- Am I interested in what the writer has to tell me?
- Would I like to know more?
- Could I be persuaded to agree with the writer, buy the product or get involved?

STRATEGIES

Skimming and scanning
Making connections
Questioning

EXPOSITIONS

In an exposition, the writer tries to persuade the reader.

An exposition is a one-sided argument. The writer puts forward a point of view and tries to persuade the reader to agree with it.

All **expositions** have the same basic structure and language features.

STRUCTURE

Introduction	The writer states his or her own point of view on a topic.
List of arguments	Each paragraph presents an argument with supporting evidence.
Conclusion	This sums up main points. Future action may be suggested.

FEATURES

- written in present tense
- may use technical words to give weight to the argument
- may include data and quotes from 'experts'
- uses emotive language to influence the feelings of the reader
- uses modal verbs to say what might, can or should happen (could, must, will, may)
- uses modifiers to weaken or soften the message (perhaps, possibly, quite, almost)
- uses intensifiers to strengthen the message (absolutely, definitely, really, most)
- uses conjunctions (if, because, so, therefore)

Think of an exposition as a big list of arguments, with strong arguments followed by weaker ones. Note how the writer connects their ideas through cause and effect, by comparing and contrasting, and by posing problems and offering solutions.

(See Top-level structure pp. 23–26)

HOW DOES AN EXPOSITION 'WORK'?

'Bring a Bag of Books to School' campaign

Are you poor? Have you ever been hungry? Most of us would probably say no to these questions. But there are hundreds of thousands of children across the world who don't have enough to eat every day and can't afford to go to school. We can help make a difference to their lives by raising money through the 'Bring a Bag of Books to School' campaign.

Introduction

Point of view

The campaign is the brainchild of our school captain, Josh Hart, and we must all get behind him to make it a huge success. The idea is that you fill a bag with books your family no longer wants and bring your bag of books to school. All the books collected will be sold at a big 'Bag a Bargain Book Sale' in the Assembly Hall on April 1 and 2.

Argument 1

The campaign kicks off on February 1. Volunteer mums and dads will be waiting to collect your bags of books every Monday morning in the school library. There is no limit to the number of bags you can bring. The number of books collected each week will be posted on the noticeboard at the front of the school. Josh hopes the public will get involved. He also plans to expand the campaign by inviting other schools to join us.

Argument 2

During the campaign, there will be weekly prizes, donated by the Council, for students who bring in the most books. Every student who brings in a bag of books will receive an 'I Bagged a Book' pencil. It doesn't matter if you only have one book to bring; it will make a difference to someone, somewhere.

Argument 3

Let's work together to get as many other kids involved as possible. Contact all your cousins and friends. Phone them, email them or post a message online. Ask them to drop off books at your house or at the school.

Argument 4

Remember, every book you place in a bag and bring to school will help a child in need. The money we raise will buy food, clothing, clean drinking water, pencils, paper and books. So, let's all work together to make this campaign a huge success!

Conclusion

Read the 'Bring a Bag of Books to School' campaign text and think about how these ideas are connected.

Example: *Are you poor? Have you ever been hungry? [CONTRASTING] Most of us would probably say no.*

1. There are children who don't get enough to eat every day [......] we can raise money through our 'Bring a Bag of Books to School' campaign. [......]

2. Every student who brings in a bag of books [......] will receive an 'I Bagged a Book' pencil. [......]

3. Every book you place in a bag [......] will help a child in need. [......]

4. The money we raise [......] will buy food, clothing and clean drinking water. [......]

Try this

Look over the 'Bring a Bag of Books to School' campaign text and give your responses.

1. What catchy phrases have been used to 'sell' the idea of the campaign?

2. What data is included to support the argument for this campaign?

3. Give a brief summary of the 'Bring a Bag of Books to School' campaign.

4. Would you be persuaded to join the campaign?

5. Rate the strength of each argument by placing an X on the line between Weak and Strong.

    Argument 1   Weak _____ Strong

    Argument 2   Weak _____ Strong

    Argument 3   Weak _____ Strong

    Argument 4   Weak _____ Strong

CHECK YOUR UNDERSTANDING

Literal

* Why did Josh launch this campaign?
* What will all participants in the campaign receive?

Right there on the page

Inferential

* How long will the campaign run?
* Why would the number of books collected be posted each week on the noticeboard?

Reading between the lines

Personal

* Do you think a campaign like this could help children in need? Give reasons.
* How do you think going to school would help these children?

Thinking about things

NEW

Glintz

The name on everyone's lips

For teeth that are whiter and a smile that's brighter!

A WORD ABOUT ADVERTISING

The purpose of **advertising** is to sell products and services. Advertisements are designed to attract attention, so they are usually colourful and appealing. If viewed on television, they are often spoken by on-screen or off-screen actors; and accompanied by movement and catchy slogans, jingles or music. Advertisements are very persuasive and greatly influence what we think and what we buy.

Advertisements are built around the following structures:

- **Problem and solution**
  Are cockroaches a problem? You need *Zero Tolerance,* the spray to stop pests dead in their tracks. Buy now and save $5!

- **Compare and contrast**
  For the ride of your life, buy a *Talisman* bike. It is stronger and lighter than most other bikes, and will outlast and outperform any other brand. Now only $250 with a free helmet.

- **Cause and effect**
  Your teeth will be whiter and your smile brighter when you switch to *Glintz,* the new minty toothpaste gel from *BBs.*

- **List (of attributes)**
  This *Chef's Little Helper* can do almost anything in the kitchen. It slices, dices, chops, cuts, grates and peels. Get the help you need for only $29.95, while stocks last.

Reader beware!

You need to understand that much advertising is based on **opinion** rather than **fact**. Indeed, some claims are blatantly false, such as in advertisements that promise you will look, feel or perform better 'in as little as seven days' by using a particular product.

DISCUSSIONS

A discussion argues for and against an issue.

A discussion is a two-sided argument. The writer presents arguments both for and against an issue. The reader evaluates the opposing arguments and makes an informed decision as to which point of view to support.

Discussions can be simple chats about books read or movies seen; or they may deal with more complex issues through political debates, or TV and radio interviews.

All **discussions** have the same basic structure and language features.

STRUCTURE

Introduction	The writer introduces the topic or issue to be discussed.
Arguments for	Each paragraph presents an argument with evidence to support it.
Arguments against	Each paragraph presents an argument with evidence to support it.
Conclusion	This sums up the main points and recommends action.

FEATURES
- written in present tense
- may use technical words to give weight to an argument
- may include data and quotes from 'experts'
- uses emotive language to influence the feelings of the reader
- uses evaluative language
- uses modal verbs to say what might, can or should happen (could, must, will, may)
- uses modifiers to weaken or soften the message (perhaps, possibly, quite, almost)
- uses intensifiers to strengthen the message (absolutely, definitely, really, most)
- uses conjunctions (if, because, so, therefore)

Think of a discussion as a big list of arguments both for and against a topic or issue. Note how the writer connects their ideas through cause and effect, by comparing and contrasting, and by posing problems and offering solutions.

(See Top-level structure pp. 23–26)

HOW DOES A DISCUSSION 'WORK'?

The Hour That Divides the Nation

For six months of the year, many Australians operate under Daylight Saving Time (DST). In October, they put their clocks forward one hour. This gives them more daylight time at the end of the day during the summer months. Queensland is an exception, keeping standard time all year round. Some believe DST has great social and health benefits, while others think it is unnatural and unnecessary. The nation remains divided on the issue.

Introduction

Points of view

DST was introduced to save energy. A lot of electricity is used to power lights, appliances and electronic equipment in the home. More daylight at the end of the day encourages people to stay outdoors longer and, therefore, use less electricity after dark. Sporting teams can train in daylight and avoid the high cost of night lighting.

The health benefits of DST are enormous. Workers have more daylight hours at the end of the day to enjoy outdoor activities such as walking, cycling, cricket, skateboarding and kite surfing. Clubs and sporting groups can get together to play games or pursue hobbies.

DST has great social and economic benefits. Families have more time to spend together at the end of the school and working day. Friends can meet for chats in outdoor cafes and coffee shops. Tourists enjoy longer hours of sightseeing, while restaurants benefit from the extra afternoon trade.

Arguments for

The case against DST is a strong one. Queensland, for example, is hot and sub-tropical, so an extra hour at the end of the working day would not be beneficial to health. Because of the heat, exercise could lead to problems such as sunburn, dehydration and heat exhaustion.

There are a number of other arguments against DST. For many farmers, DST means an extra hour of working in early morning darkness. For parents, DST causes difficulties getting babies and young children to sleep while it is still daylight. The difference in time from one state to another causes confusion and many people blame DST for the loss of business.

Arguments against

DST has been both praised and criticised. Adding daylight to evenings benefits the retail and sports industries, but can cause problems for parents, farmers, and the staging of evening entertainment such as fireworks shows. Perhaps, one day, you will be called upon to vote for or against DST. How will you vote?

Conclusion

Read the text and think about how these ideas are connected.

Example: They put their clocks forward one hour. [CAUSE] This gives them more daylight time at the end of the day. [EFFECT]

1. Some believe DST has great social and health benefits [......] while others think it is unnatural and unnecessary.
2. Because of the heat, exercise [......] could lead to problems. [......]
3. DST [......] causes difficulties getting babies and young children to sleep. [......]
4. The difference in time from one state to another [......] causes confusion. [......]
5. Many people blame DST [......] for the loss of business. [......]
6. Adding daylight to evenings benefits the retail and sports industries [......] but can cause problems for parents and farmers.

Try this

CHECK YOUR UNDERSTANDING

Literal

* When does DST begin?

* Why do farmers object to DST?

Right there on the page

Inferential

* If it is 9:00 am in Queensland, what time is it in NSW during DST?
* Why might young children find it difficult to get to sleep during DST?

Reading between the lines

Personal

* Why do you think DST is in summer and not winter?

* Do you think DST is necessary? Give reasons for your answer.

Thinking about things

HOW DO I MAKE PERSONAL MEANING?

We are constantly bombarded by persuasive texts, especially advertisements. It is important, therefore, that we evaluate what we read and reflect on what these texts mean to us personally.

Here are some questions to ask yourself about persuasive texts:

* What is the author's true purpose?
* Are the author's claims accurate?
* Do I accept the author's point of view?
* How will I respond to what I've read?
* Whose side of the argument do I agree with?
* Has this made me think or behave differently?

HOW DO I ORGANISE INFORMATION?

You will often be asked to research a topic and present the findings in your own words by way of an oral presentation, a project, a summary, a PowerPoint presentation and so on. The first step is to record information in such a way that you can use it later to prepare your presentation.

Graphic organisers are a way of representing information visually. They help you to think about and summarise the big ideas. Here are some examples:

Main idea

Details

Use **outlines** to represent the main idea and supporting details.

First World War

1914

Use **timelines** to represent things happening over time.

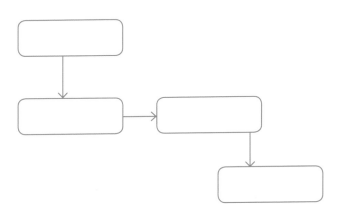

Use **flow charts** to show things, events or processes happening in order.

Use **retrieval charts** to show cause and effect OR problem and solution relationships.

Use **tables** to show comparison or to contrast data.

POPULATION	1994	2004	2014
Brisbane			
Sydney			
Melbourne			

Use **graphs** to compare or contrast data.

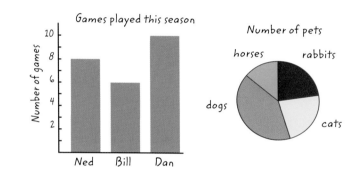

Use **labelled diagrams** to show parts of a whole.

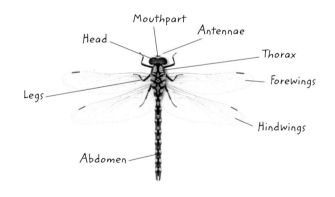

Use **cutaways** to show an inside view.

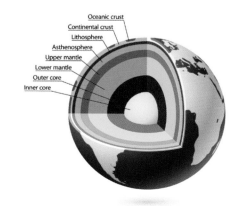

Use **graphic outlines** to show whole–part relationships.

The Frog

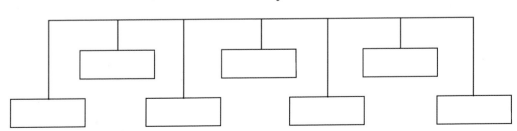

Use **graphic outlines** to show class–member relationships.

Forest products

Timber   Honey

Page

3 How do we make meaning?
- There are speech bubbles.
- One is speaking to the other face-to-face.
- They name each other.
- DJ is like a nickname. It is the short form of his real name.
- DJ
- Their holidays
- Off the north Queensland coast; the sport of swimming with a breathing tube and face mask
- Excited/pleased/happy
- Unhappy that he's not doing anything new and exciting like DJ
- Answers will vary.

5 Similes
1. like the wind
2. like a fish out of water
3. as crisp as cornflakes
4. like saucers; as white as a sheet

6 Metaphors
1. He was caught committing a crime.
2. Jones doesn't have any acceptable excuses.
3. It's time Benson made a greater effort.

12 Signs
Wheelchair access; toilets; no dogs allowed; escalator (moving staircase); shared path for walkers and bike riders; no smoking

Curves ahead (or winding road); go (green), get ready to stop (yellow), stop (red); 60 kph speed limit; road slippery when wet; road work ahead; stop

15 Comprehending non-verbal texts
(clockwise from top left) I don't know; not happy; tired; winner

19 Inferential comprehension: Pronouns
Lena's father enters the room. "Quickly Pytherius, Marco, **you** *(Pytherius and Marco)* must get to the boat," **he** *(Lena's father)* says softly. "**You** *(Pytherius and*

Page

Marco) must get away before the sun comes up or the soldiers will see **you** *(Pytherius and Marco)*."

Pytherius thanks **him** *(Lena's father)* and the two men hurry to the boat, hoping the soldiers won't see **them** *(Pytherius and Marco)*.

19 Inferential comprehension: Conclusions
1. He feels nervous.
2. He was very frightened.
3. The room is becoming brighter.

20 Inferential comprehension: Signs and symbols
one way street; no food or drink allowed; roundabout; no parking; look out for kangaroos

information; exit; first aid (medical); flammable; elevator

24 Cause and effect
1. A grasshopper has strong back legs [CAUSE] so it can leap long distances. [EFFECT]
2. Many homes have been destroyed [EFFECT] as a result of the recent bushfires. [CAUSE]
3. The big drop in elephant numbers [EFFECT] is largely due to the poaching of ivory. [CAUSE]
4. If sand is heated to a very high temperature [CAUSE] it will melt into glass. [EFFECT]
5. When the earthquake struck, [CAUSE] hundreds of homes crumbled to the ground. [EFFECT]

25 Compare and contrast
1. contrast
2. compare
3. contrast
4. compare
5. contrast

29 Substitution and ellipsis

Mr Webb divided us into small groups. He explained that we would be doing a series of different maths activities. **Some of them** *(maths activities)* would be easier than **others** *(maths activities)* and points would be awarded for successfully completing each **one** *(maths activity)*. Each small group would move from one activity to **another** *(maths activity)* and attempt to complete as many *(activities)* as possible in one hour.

34 Word chains

Clothes should be loose and comfortable. **Shorts** are ideal. Wear a **T-shirt** and take a **sweater** in case the weather turns cold. **Underclothing** is best made of cotton, as it absorbs perspiration well. Remember, you must always wear a **helmet** for safety. In winter, you may need **gloves** to keep your hands warm. Always carry something to protect you from the rain. A light **raincoat** is ideal. Always wear **brightly coloured clothes** or **luminous socks** so that you are clearly visible to other traffic.

41 Pronoun reference

Pytherius steps forward. "**I** *(Pytherius)* am Pytherius and this is Marco, son of Mykos, a nobleman from Athena," **he** *(Pytherius)* says.
"**I** *(Lena)* don't care who **you** *(Pytherius)* are, or whose son **he** *(Marco)* is," Lena says coldly, **her** *(Lena)* arrow pointed at Marco. "**You** *(Pytherius)* are on **my** *(Lena)* father's land."

42 Dialogue

Marco — angry, impetuous, brave. He doesn't like Karim and wants to get rid of him.
Karim — a bully who wants his own way and treats people badly.
Miranda — frightened, timid. She is scared of Karim and what he might do.
Marco — angry, protective of Lena. He's ready to face the bully, Karim.
Marco's father — older and wiser. He tries to caution Marco not to do anything foolish.

45 Predicting

Answers will vary. *Examples:*
1. They walk back to Athena.
Marco teaches Pytherius how to ride.
They ask someone to take them there by cart.
2. There is a robber hiding in the room and he steals the urn.
Someone is trapped and doesn't know how to get out of the room.

46 Inferring

Conclusion: Spring had arrived and the weather was warm again.
Conclusion: Jem was lost.

55 Fact or opinion?

1. Fact
2. Fact
3. Opinion
4. Fact
5. Opinion

59 Paragraphs

Waste materials can contaminate the soil.

65 Reports: Check your understanding

Literal
- Similarities: Emus and ostriches both have long, thin necks; they are flightless birds; they have two strong, powerful legs; they have feathers.
  Differences: An emu is neither as big nor as heavy as an ostrich.
- An emu defends itself by kicking, jumping, running and swerving.

Inferential
- They are big and heavy and cannot fly.
- To keep the eggs warm until they hatch.

Personal
Answers will vary. *Examples:*
- They might eat their crops.
- The emu is not found in any other country but Australia.

68 Recounts: Main idea

Paragraph 1: Pompeii was a thriving city close to Mt Vesuvius.

Paragraph 2: Vesuvius erupted, raining pumice stones down on the city.

Paragraph 3: The ash buried the city and many of its people.

Paragraph 4: People can visit the now-excavated city.

68 Recounts: Connecting ideas

1. Vesuvius began to erupt [CAUSE] pellets of pumice rained down on the city [EFFECT]
2. A rain of fine, volcanic ash began [CAUSE] leaving the city completely buried [EFFECT]
3. The city was unearthed [CAUSE] thousands of tourists can walk along the pathways [EFFECT]

69 Recounts: Timeline

Mount Vesuvius erupts: 14 August 79 AD
Pompeii buried: 17 August 79 AD
Traces of city found: 1599
Excavation begins: 1748

69 Recounts: Check your understanding

Literal
- On the shores of the Bay of Naples in Italy
- Ovens, cooking pots, mosaics, and bronze and marble statues

Inferential
- The base of the mountain
- About 2000

Personal
Answers will vary. *Examples:*
- They show what people were like and how they lived.
- To keep out any enemies

71 Procedures: Check your understanding

Literal
- Rice Bubbles
- A type of vegetable fat made from coconut

Inferential
- So you can mix all the dry ingredients together.
- Tablespoons

Personal
Answers will vary. *Examples:*
- At a party
- No. It contains a lot of sugar and fat.

73 Procedures: The power of peas

1. Fill the jar with dried peas or beans.
2. Tap the jar lightly to settle the seeds snugly.
3. Add more seeds until the jar is full.
4. Pour water into the jar until you have filled it completely.
5. Screw the lid on tightly.
6. Place the jar in a bucket and leave overnight.

76 Explanations: Connecting ideas

1. Unlike any other insect [CONTRASTING] it has scales on its wings.
2. It grows so fast [CAUSE] that it grows out of its skin several times. [EFFECT]
3. Unlike the caterpillar [CONTRASTING] the butterfly has many eyes, long legs and long antennae.
4. The female butterfly lay her eggs [CAUSE] the process starts all over again. [EFFECT]

76 Explanations: Check your understanding

Literal
- It has scales on its wings.
- The caterpillar is changing into a butterfly.

Inferential
- On the trunk of a tree
- The insect breaks out of its chrysalis.

Personal
- Answers will vary.
- Answers will vary.
Example: They chew holes in leaves and flowers.

76 Explanations: What is the water cycle?
1. The sun heats water and turns it into vapour.
2. As the vapour rises, it cools and forms clouds.
3. Drops of water join together and fall as rain.

81 Expositions: Connecting ideas
1. There are children who don't get enough to eat every day [PROBLEM] we can raise money through our 'Bring a Bag of Books to School' campaign. [SOLUTION]
2. Every student who brings in a bag of books [CAUSE] will receive an 'I Bagged a Book' pencil. [EFFECT]
3. Every book you place in the bag [CAUSE] will help a child in need. [EFFECT]
4. The money we raise [CAUSE] will buy food, clothing and clean drinking water. [EFFECT]

81 Expositions: Responses
1. 'Bring a Bag of Books to School'; 'Bag a Bargain Book Sale'; 'I Bagged a Book'
2. Hundreds of thousands of children don't get enough to eat every day. They can't afford to go to school.
3. Students are asked to bring books to school to be sold at a book sale. The money raised will go towards helping needy children.
4. Answers will vary.
5. Answers will vary

81 Expositions: Check your understanding
Literal
- To raise money for needy children
- An 'I Bagged a Book' pencil
Inferential
- Two months (1 February to 2 April)
- To encourage the public to join the campaign

Personal
- Answers will vary.
- Answers will vary.
Example: They would learn to read and write, and be able to get a job later on.

85 Discussions: Connecting ideas
1. Some believe DST has great social and health benefits [CONTRASTING] while others think it is unnatural and unnecessary.
2. Because of the heat, exercise [CAUSE] could lead to problems. [EFFECT]
3. DST [CAUSE] causes difficulties getting babies and young children to sleep. [EFFECT]
4. The difference in time from one state to another [CAUSE] causes confusion. [EFFECT]
5. Many people blame DST [CAUSE] for the loss of business. [EFFECT]
6. Adding daylight to evenings benefits the retail and sports industries [CONTRASTING] but can cause problems for parents and farmers.

85 Discussions: Check your understanding
Literal
- October
- They have to work for an hour in the early morning darkness.
Inferential
- 10:00 am
- It is still light when they go to bed.
Personal
- There are more hours of daylight in summer.
- Answers will vary.

GLOSSARY

abstract (symbol)	A symbol that denotes an idea, emotion, feeling or quality. *dove = peace; heart = love*
actor	A person who plays a character in a play, movie or TV program.
adjective	A word that describes a noun. **rosy** *cheeks,* **noisy** *children,* **exciting** *game*
adverb	A word that adds meaning to a verb. *shouted* **loudly**, *come* **here**, *speak* **quietly**
advertising	Text designed to entice people to buy goods or services.
antonym	A word opposite in meaning to another. *long, short; sea, sky; win, lose; hot, cold*
app (application)	Application software. A mobile app is specific, while a computer program is more general.
articles	The words **a** (or **an**) and **the.** They introduce nouns and noun groups. **a** *cloudy, wet day;* **an** *egg;* **the** *cat*
background (photo)	People or objects behind the main subject in a photo.
body language	Postures, gestures and facial expressions that show how we are thinking and feeling.
braille	Raised dots that blind people can read through touch.
cadence	The rhythmic rise and fall of sound in your speaking voice.
camera angle	The point from which a photo is taken. *high, low, eye-level*
caption	An explanation for a photo or illustration.
causal list	A list where one event or process leads to another, such as an explanation. *Wheat is made into flour. Flour is made into bread.*
cause and effect	Where one thing causes another to happen. *The match was cancelled because it rained.*
chronological order	Events that follow each other in time.
clause	A group of words with a subject and something to say about the subject.
coda	The final part of a narrative.
coherent	Ideas are connected in such a way that they can be easily understood.
cohesion	The way text 'sticks' together, i.e. the ideas are connected in a meaningful way.
cohesive ties	Devices used to join ideas together. *pronoun reference, repetition, conjunctions*

colloquialism	Everyday expressions we use when chatting. *Jack's a whizz at maths. Buzz off Fred.*
comma	A punctuation mark (,) used to indicate separate phrases, clauses or items in a list.
compare and contrast	Explains how things are the same (compare) or different (contrast).
composition (photo)	The way objects or people are placed within the frame of the lens.
comprehension	The process of making meaning from spoken, written, visual, non-verbal or multimodal texts.
computer	An electronic device that processes data through the use of programs.
concise	To give clear information in few words.
conjunctions	Words that join ideas together. They can be **coordinating**, **correlative** or **subordinating**.
contents	A list of the topics covered in a book.
context	The situation or setting where language takes place.
conventional (symbol)	The use of a symbol that everyone understands. *$ = dollar, % = per cent*
correlative conjunctions	Conjunctions that are used in pairs. *I don't know **whether** to go to the skate park **or** go to the movies.*
costume	Clothing and other items worn by actors to show a particular time period; or a character's culture, personality or status.
cultural context	The influence of culture on how we communicate with others.
cultural group	A group of people who share a common social and cultural experience, ethnicity, ancestry, heritage, and language.
culture	Skills, arts, beliefs and customs passed from one generation to the next.
cutaway	A diagram used to show an inside view of an image.
definite article	The word **the** used before a noun, where the noun is already known (definite).
detail	A small part relating to or supporting the main ideas of the text.
diagram	A drawing that shows the parts of something or how something works.
dialogue	Conversation between two or more people.
directions	Guidance on how to get somewhere or how to carry out a task. *Heating Soup in a Microwave*
discussion	A two-sided argument with arguments both **for** and **against** an issue.
e-reader	A portable electronic device that can be used to read books or other text in a digital format.

editing (movie)	Selecting scenes and putting them together with a soundtrack to make a movie.
ellipsis	The omission of one or two words from a sentence without loss of meaning. It may be indicated by a series of dots. (...)
enunciate	To pronounce words in a very particular and distinctive way.
euphemism	A vague or indirect expression used to avoid being blunt or offensive. *die = **pass away***
evaluation	To make a judgement about something.
explanation	Tells us how and why things work or happen. *What is a rainbow? Why does a volcano erupt?*
explicit (meaning)	When words mean what they say and the meaning is clear.
exposition	A one-sided argument to persuade readers to a particular point of view.
fact	A true statement about a topic that can be proven.
fade-in	When a scene gradually comes into view on a TV or movie screen.
fiction	Narratives that are not true but are created from the imagination.
figurative language	Text that contains figures of speech, especially metaphors.
figure of speech	Expressive use of language where the meaning is not literal. *simile, metaphor*
flashback	A part of a story (or movie) that shows an event that happened at an earlier time.
flow chart	A detailed diagram that shows how one process leads to another. *Farm to Table: Making Bread*
fluently	To speak or write very easily or in a flowing way.
foreground (photo)	The part of the picture closest to the viewer. In photos, the subject is usually in the foreground.
format	The general appearance of a book. *number of pages, font, margins, paper, size, shape*
gesture	Movement or position of the hand, head, face or body to portray an emotion, opinion or idea.
glossary	A list of important words in alphabetical order and their meanings, usually found at the back of a book.
grammar	An arrangement of words into 'pieces of language' that we can recognise and understand.
graph	A diagram using dots, lines or bars that shows the relationship between two or more things.
graphic designer	A person who represents information in a visual form. *graph, flow chart*

graphic organiser	A device used to represent information visually. *timeline, flow chart, graph, table*
graphic outline	A diagram with headings and subheadings, and branches connecting them in groups of related information.
graphic representation	Information presented in visual form. *timeline, flow chart, graph, diagram, cutaway*
icon (computer)	A picture on a digital screen that represents programs or applications.
illustration	Pictures used in a book to interpret the story. Illustrations clarify, and often extend, the meaning.
illustrator	A person who depicts scenes from a story to clarify or extend the meaning.
image	A representation of reality produced by a photographer, artist or illustrator.
imaginative text	Stories that come out of the imagination and are not true.
imperative verb	An order or command. *Open the door. Close the window.*
implied (meaning)	When words don't mean exactly what they say and the meaning must be worked out by using the context.
indefinite article	The word **a** (or **an**) used before a noun, where the noun is unknown (indefinite).
index	A list in alphabetical order containing the pages where you can find information in a book. It is more detailed than the contents page.
inferential comprehension	When the words don't mean exactly what they say and the meaning is implied.
inferring	Discovering meaning by piecing together bits of information. *He looked at the clock and ran.*
informal	A casual, relaxed way of speaking and writing. It includes slang and colloquialisms. *G'day mate!*
information	Facts or knowledge about a particular subject.
information text	Any text whose purpose is to inform. *reports, brochures, websites, TV guides, manuals*
instructions	A list of steps to follow to make or do something. *recipe, procedure*
jargon	A language specific to a trade, profession or group e.g. plumbers, doctors, divers, musicians.
language	Verbal and non-verbal means of communication through speech, words, pictures, signs and symbols.
language features	The 'working parts' of a text. *tense, person, vocabulary, photos, illustrations, diagrams*
layout	The way text and pictures are positioned on a page.

lens (camera)	A part of a camera (a piece of glass) used to focus the image to take a photo.
lighting	Using light to give different effects in photos or movies. *bright, side, backlit*
listing	A way of organising ideas into lists. Many texts (such as recounts) are just a big list of ideas or events.
literal (meaning)	When information is explicit in the text and words mean what they say.
literal comprehension	When we understand because the words mean what they say. *We ate a pizza for lunch.*
main idea	The central idea or event in a paragraph.
making connections	Connecting what you know from other books and experiences with what you are now reading.
making meaning	The process of 'reading' the world around us so that we can understand it and learn how to live in it.
medium (photography)	The type of format used to create the photograph. *film, digital, colour, black and white*
metaphor	A word or phrase that doesn't mean what it says. *His hair stood on end. That was a close shave.*
monitoring	The process of keeping a careful check on what you are reading so that it continues to make sense.
movie	A story recorded visually and shown in a cinema or on TV. Also called a **film**.
moving images	Images created with a video camera or digicam, often by filmmakers or TV cameramen.
multimodal text	A text (e.g. movies, TV) that includes different modes of language such as **spoken**, **visual**, **non-verbal** or **written**.
music	A language recognised by musicians all over the world that is composed almost entirely of signs and symbols.
narrative	A story or account of events and experiences.
news ticker/crawler	A rolling display of headlines and other items of news at the bottom of a TV screen.
non-fiction text	Text that deals with, or has opinions about, facts and reality.
non-verbal language	Communication through gestures, postures, facial expressions and signs.
noun	A word that names a person, animal, place or thing. *dentist, zebra, city, bicycle*
opinion	What someone *thinks* about a topic. It may or may not be true and cannot be proven.
outline	A graphic organiser that represents the main idea and supporting details of a text.

paragraph	A segment of text (usually less than 10 sentences), grouped around a main idea.
personal	Something related to an individual's own feelings or experiences.
personal comprehension	When we evaluate a text and think about what it has meant to us personally.
personification	Treating animals, objects and ideas as if they are people. *Dawn crept in with chilly fingers.*
persuasive text	Text designed to influence the reader's thinking on a particular topic or issue.
photograph	Still images produced by a camera.
photographer	A person who uses cameras to produce still images in the form of photographs.
phrase	A group of words containing a noun or pronoun but no verb.
pitch	The *high* and *low* sounds of the voice.
play	A story written to be performed onstage by actors, and told through dialogue and movement.
poetry	Writing set out in a certain way, often with lines that match in length, rhythm or rhyme.
point of view	The ideas and attitude you have toward a particular topic or issue.
predict	To make a statement about what might happen in the future.
predicting	Guessing what a text might be about, or thinking about what might happen next or later on, based on what we already know.
preposition	A word used to position people and things. *in the park, **over** the hill, **after** the game*
previewing	Browsing through the text to get a sense of the story.
principal (main) clause	A clause that consists of one complete idea.
problem and solution	Ideas organised around a problem and how it might be solved.
procedure	A sequence of instructions to be followed to carry out a task. *Using a Coin-Operated Machine*
pronoun	A word used instead of a noun. *Tom, **he**, **him**; Bella, **she**, **her**; bird, **it**; students, **they**, **them***
pronoun reference	The use of pronouns to refer backwards (and forwards) to the nouns they replace.
prop	Any object used as part of a stage or movie setting, excluding the scenery.
pun	A play on words. *It's pointless to write with a broken pencil. Do you know anyone hooked on fishing?*

punctuation	Marks used in writing to make meaning clear. *commas, full stops, question marks, exclamation marks*
purpose	The reason why a writer writes, a reader reads, and a viewer watches TV or movies.
questioning	Keeping in touch with the meaning of a text by asking **Who**, **What**, **Where**, **When**, **Why** and **How**.
reading	The act of understanding the meaning of something.
recount	A type of text where you tell or write about events in chronological order. It can be **factual** or **personal**. *diary, email, historical account*
reflecting	Thinking back over a text and making judgements about the characters, plot and events.
repetition	When words, phrases or sentences are repeated so their meanings are clearly understood.
report	A type of information text where you give factual information about something. *Hot Air Balloons, Cycling, The Olympic Games*
responding	Recording your reaction to a story. *draw a character, make a mask, write to the author*
retelling	Where we tell others about our reading experience, including the main characters and events, and the problem and resolution.
retrieval chart	A graphic organiser used to visually represent relationships between ideas, such as cause and effect.
reviewing	Going back over a text to check, memorise, summarise or evaluate information, or to look for answers.
scanning	Looking for specific bits of information in a text. *dates, key words, numbers, names of people/places*
scenery	The background features onstage that give a sense of place or character.
script	The written text of a play, a movie, or a TV or radio program.
sequence	Things that follow in order, one after another. Can be chronological or logical.
setting	The time or environment where the action takes place.
shoot (movie)	Filming short segments of a movie for later editing. Each segment is called a 'take'.
sign	A word or picture that shows us where things are or what to do. *You Break, You Buy!*
sign language	Used by deaf people to communicate. *finger spelling, hand shapes, gestures, facial expressions*
simile	A phrase that says how one thing is like, or similar to, another. It usually begins with **like** or **as**. *run **like** the wind; white **as** snow*

skimming	Running your eyes quickly over a text to get an idea of what it is about.
slang	Very informal words that are playful and metaphorical. *Let's hit the road. Stone the crows!*
smartphone	A mobile phone that can run applications and perform computer functions.
social context	The social situation or setting in which language occurs.
social group	Two or more people who share common characteristics such as interests, values, ethnic backgrounds or family ties.
social networking site	A website or application where people or social groups with similar interests can connect through the use of a personal profile. *Facebook, Twitter*
sound effects	Sounds used in movies to make things seem real. *clock chiming, door slamming, thunder rolling*
split-screen	When a TV screen is divided into two or more segments, with each showing different images.
stance	The point of view of the reader (**reader's stance**) or writer (**author's stance**) based on their knowledge, beliefs and experience.
strategy	A plan or method for obtaining a specific goal or result.
subject (photography)	The person, object or animal that is the focus of a photo.
subordinate (dependent) clause	Says more about the main idea in the main clause. It is linked to the main clause by a conjunction or relative pronoun.
substituting	Replacing a word so it acts in the place of another. *I'm buying a chicken. Do you want **one**?*
subtitle	The text of a dialogue translated into another language and displayed at the bottom of a TV or movie screen.
summarising	Giving a short, concise statement of the main ideas.
summary	A statement of the main ideas and relevant details of a text. It can be **visual** (*diagrams, photos, charts*) or **written**.
symbol	An image or object that has a deeper meaning. *dove = peace; $ = dollar*
synonym	A word similar in meaning to another, used to avoid too much repetition. ***say:*** *shout, cry, moan*
table (graphic organiser)	A diagram where information is organised in a series of rows and columns.
tablet (computer)	A portable computer that can run applications and perform computer functions. It uses a touchscreen instead of a keyboard and mouse.
take (movie)	Scenes of a movie or television show filmed in short segments.

text	Written, spoken, visual or non-verbal language used to convey meaning. *book, movie, sign, TV*
timeline	A type of graphic representation composed of a line marked with important events in chronological order.
time sequence	The passage of time in a story, indicated by specific words or phrases. *Later that day, Suddenly, After a while, Then*
top-level structure	The different patterns of thinking that we use to produce language. *cause/effect; compare/contrast; problem/solution; listing*
topic sentence	The main idea of a paragraph, often the first sentence.
touchscreen	An electronic display on a computer or smartphone where functions can be controlled through the use of fingers or a stylus.
transition words	Words or phrases that join ideas together in particular ways. *addition, time, place, cause and effect*
verb	A word used to tell us what people and things do, say, think and feel. *laugh, swim, believe, howl*
verbal language	Communication through spoken words.
viewing	The act of looking or seeing with the eye.
visualising	Picturing the people, actions and events in your mind as you are reading.
visuals	The picture elements of a text. *photos, illustrations, graphic representations*
vocabulary	The words speakers and writers use. They can be **technical** (subject specific) or **everyday** (common) words.
volume	The intensity of sound, ranging from **soft** (low volume) to **loud** (high volume).

INDEX